LABOUR-BASED ROAD CONSTRUCTION

LABOUR-BASED ROAD CONSTRUCTION

Edited by

PAUL LARCHER

INTERMEDIATE TECHNOLOGY PUBLICATIONS
1998

Intermediate Technology Publications
103-105 Southampton Row, London WC1B 4HH, UK

© Institute of Development Engineering 1998

A CIP record for this book is available from
the British Library

ISBN 1 85339 416 5

Typeset by Karen Betts
Designed by Rod Shaw

Printed in the UK by SRP, Exeter

Table of contents

*Prizewinning papers

Introduction

This book has been produced by the Management of Appropriate Road Technology (MART) Initiative. The aim of the project is to achieve sustainable improvements in road construction and maintenance through the optimum use of local resources and skills, the effective use of the private sector and the application of good management practices in both contracting and employing organizations. MART is funded by a Department for International Development (DFID) Technology Development and Research (TDR) grant. It is led by the Construction Enterprise Unit, Institute of Development Engineering at Loughborough University in association with Intech Associates and I. T. Transport.

The MART project will draw together expertise in labour-based technologies and the development of construction enterprises, with a view to codifying this experience in the form of a series of four guidelines covering:

○ Handtools
○ Intermediate equipment
○ Private sector development
○ Institution building.

In order to generate information on recent developments in all four categories MART ran a competition, sponsored by the British Public Works Association (BPWA) which donated prizes of £500 for the best paper in each category. The outcome of the competition was the publication of this book which contains lightly edited versions of entries received for the competition.

The competition was held in the second half of 1995 and was judged by a panel of eight members who came from a range of civil engineering backgrounds. The panel agreed that the winning papers were those written by:

○ Bill Hancox, entitled 'Intermediate equipment for labour-based roadworks' (Handtools and Intermediate equipment categories)
○ Athie Lehobo, entitled 'Transformation of the labour construction unit from an executing agency to a contract supervisory agency' (Private sector

development category)
○ John Ward, entitled 'Institution building for small-scale contractor development in South Africa' (Institution building category).

The aim of running the competition was to collect information from those with expertise in labour-based construction and contractor development. It was hoped that the use of a competition format would encourage papers from authors who would otherwise not have contributed to a research project, and would have been unlikely to have passed on their experience to a wider audience. The expertise and ideas gained from the papers will ultimately be used to assist with the preparation of a set of guidelines on contractor development.

The authors come from a range of different backgrounds and are therefore likely to have differing viewpoints on the issues involved in contractor development. The editor has not altered the opinions or arguments of the original papers, which remain those of the authors and do not necessarily represent those held by MART, DFID or BPWA. A short résumé is included about each author in order to inform the reader about the background from which each paper was written.

There are a total of twelve papers and a case study on the Winterveld Presidential Project, which relates to the two papers submitted by John Ward. It may therefore be read in conjunction with either paper.

The MART team wish to express their gratitude to all the authors who responded to the call for papers and also to the BPWA for their generosity in sponsoring the competition and contributing to the cost of producing this book.

Acronyms

BPWA	British Public Works Association
CTA	Chief Technical Adviser
CTB	Central Tender Board (Lesotho)
DFID	Department for International Development
DFR	Department of Feeder Roads (Ghana)
DFR	Durban Functional Region (South Africa)
EDP	Enterprise Development Programme (South Africa)
EU	European Union
FIDIC	International Federation of Consulting Engineers
FURMMP	Fixed Unit Rate Mechanised Maintenance Programme (Uganda)
GOL	Government of Lesotho
GTZ	Gesellschaft für Technische Zusammenarbeit
IDA	International Development Administration
ILO	International Labour Office
IYCB	Improve Your Construction Business
KFW	Kreditanstalt für Wiederaufbau
KShs	Kenyan Shillings
KTS	Kisii Training School (Kenya)
LB	Labour Based
LBCP	Labour Based Contracting Programme (Uganda)
LBCTP	Labour Based Contractor Training Project (Kenya)
LCU	Labour Construction Unit (Lesotho)
MART	Management of Appropriate Road Technology
MOPWH	Ministry of Public Works and Housing (Kenya)
MOWTC	Ministry of Works, Transport and Communications (Uganda)
MRP	Minor Roads Programme (Kenya)
NGO	Non-Governmental Organization
ODA	Overseas Development Administration (UK) (now DFID)
RARP	Rural Access Roads Programme
RDP	Reconstruction and Development Programme (South Africa)
ROCAR	Road Construction and Rehabilitation
ROMAR	Road Maintenance and Regravelling
SIDA	Swedish International Development Authority
TDR	Technology Development and Research (DFID grant)
UNDP	United Nations Development Programme

Review of the papers

A total of twelve papers were submitted to the competition, five within the Handtools and Intermediate equipment categories and seven within the Private sector development and Institution building categories. Reviews of each category and of the individual papers are given below.

Handtools and Intermediate equipment categories

Five papers were submitted covering the topics of handtools and intermediate equipment. Two papers discuss the evolution of the Kenyan 3m³ gravel trailer and towing hitches, describing some of the modifications which have been undertaken and proposing further improvements to the current design. A further two papers discuss from different perspectives the use of towed graders. One paper is written by a user, who operates a towed grader for the maintenance of the access roads in a tea plantation. The other is written by the sales director of a towed grader manufacturer and supplier. The fifth paper offers an overview of the use of handtools and intermediate equipment in India, explaining how tractor-towed or tractor-powered equipment can be used for roadworks.

Intermediate equipment for roadworks (Jim Hamper)
This paper discusses the use of a tractor and trailer combination for roadworks. The author describes the choice of tractor, indicating the potential pitfalls and reasons for choosing particular versions. The paper addresses the issues of hitch design and the problems with the current simple designs. Hamper proposes the use of an automatic pick-up hitch which may be powered from the tractor hydraulic system or operated manually. He proposes the use of a ball and socket joint, but explains that the pick-up hitch can also use a bolt and eye fixing.

The paper concludes with a section on the Kenyan 3m³ gravel trailer. The author gives an account of its development and discusses design developments and features of the version currently in use.

Note. The trailer design described in this paper forms the basis for ILO/ASIST Technical Brief No. 1: Designs and Specifications for a Standard Trailer and Hitch for labour-based roadworks, ILO-ASIST, Nairobi, Kenya.

Intermediate equipment for labour-based roadworks (Bill Hancox)

This paper discusses the author's experiences in Kenya with 3m³ gravel trailers and towing hitches. It explains how early designs were unable to withstand the rough treatment that was encountered on roadworks projects. The problems of wear experienced with the traditional towing hitches and rings are discussed, and the author's alternative is presented. Hancox also discusses the issues of material selection and fatigue testing of the towing hitches and explains the need to test the hitches both under British and ISO standards and under normal operating conditions.

The paper also discusses the evolution of the Kenyan 3m³ gravel trailer from its prototype version in 1987, describing a number of features and modifications that were successful and unsuccessful. Hancox suggests a further improvement which will lower the trailer floor height by 200mm, which will reduce the time and energy required to load and unload the trailer.

Management of appropriate road technology in India (A. Murty)

This describes the handtools and intermediate equipment used for road construction in India. It indicates that, in general, unmodified agricultural handtools are used which are supplied by the labourers themselves.

The author explains that the Central Road Research Institute (CRRI) has carried out research to identify items of tractor-towed agricultural equipment that can be used for roadworks along with their relative efficiencies. The paper describes some of the construction or maintenance tasks and the tractor-towed equipment that may be used to undertake them.

Equipment selection for rural road maintenance in developing countries (Mike Hodge)

This paper was written by Mike Hodge, the Export Manager of Simba International, and offers an unusual insight into the motivation of a manufacturer based in a developing country which has identified and exploited a market opening for simple, robust and easy-to-maintain equipment. Four types of equipment are described:

○ towed and light duty graders
○ lime stabilization equipment
○ tractor drawn dead-weight road rollers
○ towed box scrapers.

The paper describes the way in which the manufacturer sets a design brief for equipment to suit this market, and suggests useful guidelines for those responsible for equipment procurement on labour-based projects.

Intermediate equipment (Lou Wedd)

This paper discusses the road maintenance problems that the African High-lands Produce Company Ltd encountered when it switched from moving its firewood with tractors and trailers to using lorries. The author explains the reasons for the company's choice to use a tractor and towed grader rather than replace its motor grader for the maintenance of its roads.

The paper also discusses the methods and equipment that the company uses for constructing its roads in an area where murram (gravel/laterite) is unavailable. It indicates that the old motor grader has been used in parallel with the new towed grader. Wedd states that the towed grader is cheaper to run and operate and can be used in more confined areas. Although the towed grader has a significantly higher work-rate and lower running costs, the two cannot be directly compared due to their relative ages.

The author concludes with the observations that anti-flip hitches are preferable to swinging tow bars or pickup hitches, and that weight transfer across the hitch does not seem to offer any advantages.

Private sector development and Institution building categories

Six of the seven papers submitted to the competition describe a particular country's contractor-development programme, with the seventh discussing more general issues drawing on material from several different countries. The countries covered in detail include: Ghana, Kenya, Lesotho, South Africa and Uganda. In each of these papers the author has described the evolution of the country's contractor-development programme from its initial stages through to the present. Although each programme has been developed individually in each country, a number of similar lessons can be drawn from the experiences gained on the projects.

Each development programme found that there were sufficient contractors available to be included in the programmes, often with capable technical abilities. However, every programme either found, or correctly assumed, that the contractors lacked construction and business management experience. Consequently a significant proportion of each project consisted of a contractor-training programme. These training programmes included an element of technical training but they also developed contractors' ability to tender and bid for work. The detailed format varied between countries but fell into two general categories:

○ *Tiered bidding structure.* Before the contractors left the training programme and competed in the 'open market' they went through a multi-level bidding exercise. At each level the maximum allowable contract price and the performance guarantees offered by the contractor increased. Contractors are generally allowed to bid for contracts only at the level that they have currently reached, thus protecting newer businesses from the well-established.

○ *Fixed unit rate contracts:* Contractors undertake work at a fixed unit rate, allowing them to establish their businesses before having to compete for work by open competitive tendering.

All the papers describe the development of the programmes as starting with an initial pilot phase, usually in one area of the country. It is also stressed in some papers, and apparent from the others, that the expansion of the programme must be undertaken at a rate that the associated services (e.g. finance or training) can support. The papers also highlight the importance of the changes required in government departments in order to administer the contracts. New groups within the existing departments should be formed and trained in contract administration techniques. The capacity of these groups should increase at a similar rate to the number of private contractors and/or contracts offered.

Each paper discusses the issues of contractor finance and equipment – however, there are no clear similarities in approach between projects. Project details range from large financial loans to small individual commitments, and from no project equipment provision to a significant equipment fleet.

Labour-based roadworks: Private sector development (E. Ashong)

This paper is a factual account of the Ghanaian labour-based road programme, part of the Ghanaian Development Programme, which commenced in 1986. Ashong describes the different stages of the project from the pilot scheme in 1987 to the later dissemination stages. The paper also describes in some detail the contractor selection and training programme associated with the project.

Ashong concludes with four recommendations for the continuation of the scheme:

○ Ensure that there is enough supervisory capacity within the executing agency.
○ Carry out follow-up training.
○ Geographical expansion should be gradual and matched with the available man-power and/or logistics ability.
○ Ensure that the project does not become politically propelled.

Experiences and lessons regarding the introduction of local contractor operations and appropriate technology roadworks in a number of countries (Michael Broadbent)

This paper examines, through case studies, some of the problems that countries have experienced when adopting a labour-based roadworks programme. Broadbent states that little change has occurred in labour-based techniques since their inception 20 years ago, and that there have been no major breakthroughs that would allow labour-based techniques to be carried out on a sustainable basis.

The paper discusses the 'recipe method' of construction which precludes initial studies and design; a rural road may simply be specified as to be built from A to B. This allows all the available money to be channelled into the costs of building the road, which, it may be argued, produces a cost-effective solution. However, the author also points out that the contractor does not have a design for which to provide a price estimate, and the client cannot specify their full requirements.

Four case studies are described, with specific problems and pitfalls discussed:

○ *The Caribbean:* The FIDIC contract was specified by the donor agency. Unfortunately, the contractors involved in the programme made no effort to understand their obligations under the contract, despite the provision of a training scheme. The industry reacted with a negative response to the contract, which may have resulted in a decrease in the capacity and capability of the industry.

○ *The Far East:* This case study looks at work carried out simultaneously by three different methods, due to the inability of labour-based methods to meet demand. Methods used comprised force account using labour-based techniques or old plant, and the traditional private sector capacity.

○ *East Africa:* Different labour-based methods have been tried here. This case study examines the methods which include force account, private sector, lengthmen and labour-based work combined with lease hire agreements for intermediate technology equipment.

○ *Other countries:* Contractor finance and risk are examined in the Indian subcontinent and in West Africa.

The author ends the paper with a strategy for expanding labour-based private sector construction, which may be considered as a list of recommendations and requirements.

Labour-based contractor training project (LBCTP) in Kenya (F. Karanja)

The LBCTP is a programme complementary to the minor roads programme (MRP), set up to allow work on the MRP to be carried out by small-scale private contractors rather than by force account. The paper describes the project from its implementation, in 1991, to the completion of the training programme by the first group of contractors. Karanja gives a great deal of information regarding the selection and recruiting of suitable contractors.

The paper indicates that there are sufficient suitable contractors for the programme; however, there is a dearth of suitable foremen/supervisors. The training project has often found it necessary to train individual foremen and allow them to be recruited by the trained contractors.

Karanja explains that the number of small-scale contractors may be increased by:

○ changing from the lengthmen system to using contractors
○ preparation of simple contract documents
○ training suitable personnel

and that labour-based construction can be increased by:

○ a comprehensive review of the quantities and types of roadworks carried out in the Roads Department each year
○ classification of roadworks to indicate those which need to be done under equipment-based methods, mix of equipment and labour or labour-based methods
○ a move away from force account systems to contracting systems
○ setting up a Construction Bank to assist new local contractors in the country.

Transformation of the Labour Construction Unit from an executing agency to a contract supervisory agency (Athie Lehobo)
This paper examines how the Labour Construction Unit (LCU) in Lesotho is adapting its road maintenance programme from a force account labour system to a small-scale private contractor system. Lehobo, the ex-chief engineer of the LCU, introduces the problems that were present before the system was changed, and describes how the project was financed.

There are two main sections to the paper, which enter into great detail on how the project was implemented. The first section deals with the lack of suitable contractors, how candidates were recruited, trained and the initial contracts awarded and carried out. The second section describes the changes carried out within the LCU to allow them to become a part-supervisory agency (road construction is still currently carried out by force account).

Lehobo critically analyses the problems encountered, and changes made, during the first two years of this 20-year programme. The paper concludes with a section on the lessons learned, and hence recommendations for the continuation of the project.

Commitment and initiatives of the Ugandan government to establishing a sustainable capacity for road maintenance using local small-scale contractors (William Musumba)
The author is the Chief Road Maintenance Engineer for the Ugandan government. In this paper he discusses two of the Ugandan government-financed labour-based road initiatives; The Labour-Based Contracting Programme (LBCP) and the Fixed Unit Rate Mechanized Maintenance Programme (FURMMP).

The LBCP was initiated in January 1993 and is concerned with road maintenance. The paper examines the planning, inception, training and running of the programme, which utilizes lengthmen and small gangs (of approximately 10 men), to maintain 2km and 10km of road respectively. The paper concludes that the scheme has been sustainable and successful. The only main area still to be improved is the training aspects of the scheme.

FURMMP started in October 1994 to fulfil the requirement that, by the year 2000, all mechanized maintenance will be carried out under contracts. It allows small-scale contractors to carry out work without the requirements of having to prepare tenders and bids. The paper gives some details of the planning and inception of the scheme.

Annexes to the paper give examples of the contractor/lengthmen prequalification forms and worksheets used for the scheme.

From dependency to autonomy: an Afrocentric approach to small-scale contractor development in South Africa (John Ward)

This paper examines the problems facing the South African construction industry following the ending of apartheid in April 1993. It indicates that the industry is dominated by white contractors, and that there are two types of black contractor: sub-contractors who are employed by white managers (these contractors existed during apartheid), and small-scale contractors, who have recently emerged. The author points out that the training required for these two groups is different.

The paper explains the problems facing small-scale contractors, which may be summarized as:

○ Finance   – difficulty in acquiring finance
            – lack of collateral
○ Authority – different methods of investing authority
○ Training   – training black contractors tends to be very condescending
               (preventing them using their initiative)
○ Standards – construction standards are colonial and do not reflect
               African requirements.

The paper summarizes the initiatives that need to be adopted in South Africa. These may be divided into South Africa specifically and those which apply to Africa in general.

Institution building for small-scale contractor development in South Africa (John Ward)

This paper describes the role and initiatives that the contractor support agency, Khuphuka, is undertaking in the development of the construction industry in South Africa. Ward explains that Khuphuka needs to provide three types of training in order to create a sustainable development of small enterprises:

○ organizational and managerial skills to control their own development competently

○ technical skills to encourage local people to facilitate job creation opportunities
○ business skills to provide job opportunities on a self-employment basis.

The paper introduces the South African government's Enterprise Development Programme and explains how Khuphuka is developing an integrated training programme that will assist in meeting the objectives of the government's programme.

The Winterveld Presidential Project: A case study (John Ward)

The last two papers both use the Winterweld project as a case study to demonstrate the approach used to promote small-scale contractors. The object of the project is to provide a cost-effective water supply to the Winterweld area as well as developing small-scale contractors. The two key aspects of the scheme are:

○ *Contract division:* The contracts are divided up into five levels. The lowest, for new contractors, having a maximum value of about US $2,750 and no performance guarantees. The values then rise, for the more experienced contractors, to about $700,000 with performance guarantees.
○ *Training:* This is carried out in two phases. Phase one gives an introduction to contractors allowing them to submit bids for the Winterweld scheme. Phase two utilizes the ILO IYCB publications and interactive group work to equip the contractors to bid for projects elsewhere.

About the authors

W. Hancox

Bill Hancox is an independent management and engineering consultant working in overseas development and specializing in small enterprise development, rural roads and the agribusiness sectors. He has extensive experience of both labour-based and equipment-based road construction in a mechanical engineering capacity and was involved in equipment fleet management on both the Rural Access Roads Programme and Minor Roads Programme in Kenya. Additional roads experience has been gained in Uganda, Tanzania and Indonesia and he is particularly interested in the start-up of small-scale contractors.

J. Hamper

Jim Hamper is a private Canadian consultant with thirty-five years experience in the maintenance and management of equipment fleets in both the on- and off-highway sector. He has spent the last fifteen years working with various Governments and Donor Agencies in Africa assisting and advising on equipment requirements and maintenance management systems. For the last six years he has been attached to the Ministry of Public Works and Housing in Kenya as Equipment Adviser to the Rural Access and Minor Roads Programme. He presently holds the position of Superintending Engineer, Mechanical Services Unpaved Roads Branch and is based at the Roads Department Headquarters, Nairobi.

A. Murty

A. Murty is the Head of Soil Stabilisation and Rural Roads Division at the Central Road Research Institute (CRRI), India. Since joining the CRRI in 1969 he has written a number of technical papers, and undertaken applied research relating to highway and geotechnical engineering, particularly in the fields of ground improvement and control of land slides. He is the co-author of the CRRI publication; Manual for Construction and Maintenance of Low Volume Roads.

M. Hodge

Mike Hodge has been working as Export Manager for Simba International Ltd for 5 years. His main areas of responsibility are Africa and the third world. Prior to this appointment he spent a short time with Matbro after working for a large Caterpillar dealership in both the UK and Africa for 15 years, specialising in agricultural equipment.

L. A. G. Wedd

Lou Wedd has worked for The African Highlands Produce Company for 33 years. He was originally trained as a motor vehicle engineer, having worked briefly on aircraft before joining AHP. Since joining AHP he has taught himself many aspects of engineering related to the production of tea. He is a Companion of the Institution of Agricultural Engineers and an Associated Member of the Automobile Industry.

E. N. K. Ashong

E. Ashong is a senior engineer with the Department of Feeder Roads (DFR) in Ghana and one of the two pioneers of the introduction of labour-based technology to Ghana in 1986. He has worked in various capacities ranging from a Project Engineer to a Regional Engineer since joining the department in 1982 and has been the national co-ordinator of the labour-based programme since October 1992.

Mr. Ashong graduated from the University of Science and Technology in Ghana in 1982. After working for the DFR for eight years he studied for an MSc at the Technical University of Delft, Holland, returning to DFR in 1992.

M. Broadbent

Michael Broadbent is an independent consulting engineer with wide experience both in the UK and abroad. He has specialized in management of infrastructure programmes and has expertise in the planning, design, construction and maintenance of works together with organization, administration, training, technical assistance and institutional requirements of government departments.

His experience includes road and bridge engineering, covering feasibility studies; engineering design, construction and maintenance; project management and evaluation; and advising on major policy and strategic matters. This experience has been gained both on major highways as well as rural roads, with works implementation by machine-intensive or labour-based methods either under contract or by force account.

F. D. Karanja

F.D. Karanja is a Superintending Engineer (Roads) in the Roads Department of the Ministry of Public Works and Housing, Kenya. He is currently acting as a Senior Superintending Engineer in charge of Planning Evaluation and Monitoring in the Unpaved Roads Branch of the Roads Department. He completed his BSc in Civil Engineering from the University of Nairobi in 1980. Mr. Karanja has been working in the Roads Department since 1980 in various Branches including Planning, Design, Construction and Unpaved Roads. He is a Registered Engineer with the Engineers Registration Board (Kenya) and is a Corporate Member of the Institution of Engineers of Kenya.

A. Lehobo

Tlohang Athie Lehobo holds a diploma in Civil Engineering (Lesotho), a BSc in Civil Engineering (University of Manitoba, Canada) and a certificate in a Senior Management Course at post-graduate level (University of Manchester, UK).

He joined the Lesotho Public Service in 1972 as a high school leaver. He worked in the Ministry of Works and was involved with the establishment of the Labour Construction Unit (LCU) in 1977 as the most senior local field officer. Mr. Lehobo became Field and Planning Engineer and eventually the Head of the LCU, its Chief Engineer, in 1986. During his period as Chief Engineer he transformed the LCU from an organization which lacked clear responsibility and permanent status within the Government of Lesotho to a full Branch of the Ministry of Works, with responsibility for improvement and maintenance of low-volume rural roads comprising nearly 50 per cent of the national road network.

He took an early retirement and left the public service at the end of March 1993 to become a private consultant specializing in labour-based technology. However, before leaving the LCU he had initiated a project aimed at transforming the LCU from a force account executing agency to a contract supervisory agency.

W. Musumba

William Musumba is a civil engineering graduate of the University of Nairobi. He started work in the Kenyan Ministry of Works and Housing in 1976 and now holds the rank of Acting Chief Road Maintenance Engineer. He has over 16 years experience in the planning, implementation and supervision of road-related activities and has contributed to the improved maintenance practice in the Ministry of Works Transport and Communications. He headed the formulation and implementation team for the new road maintenance strategies.

Mr. Musumba has actively participated in the labour-based technology development and implementation in his country. He is in charge of the Labour-Based Contracting Programme which started through a local initiative, and has continued with minimal input from external sources. He has participated in the major ILO workshops and seminars since 1993 and has given several presentations to local workshops and seminars on labour-based technology.

J. Ward

John Ward is an independent consultant specializing in training for construction enterprises. He is currently a consultant to Khuphuka, a non governmental organization set up to help disadvantaged communities throughout KwaZulu Natal, South Africa and is also responsible for contractor training and development on the Winterveld Presidential Project. Prior to becoming an independent consultant he was an ILO Chief Technical Adviser, working in Vanuatu, South Pacific and Ghana. During the latter assignment he was responsible for the ILO Improve Your Construction Business (IYCB) project, co-writing the three IYCB handbooks and workbooks.

CHAPTER 1

Intermediate equipment for roadworks

J. Hamper

Appropriate technology

When we speak of appropriate technology as it pertains to equipment dealing with roadworks it is important that we first determine what type of works we are concerned with. While dozers and heavy graders are appropriate for some types of road work, common hand tools are appropriate for others. For the purpose of this paper we shall deal with one type of intermediate equipment that is used specifically for gravelling in labour-based road maintenance – tractors, hitches and trailers.

Equipment selection

Selection of the most appropriate units from the three mentioned above can be a difficult and controversial decision. This paper will attempt to alleviate some of those difficulties and offer some suggestions as to what could be the most appropriate choices. With regards to tractors, this choice should be fairly easy once you establish the size required and the most suitable make and model for the area concerned. Price alone should not be the determining factor. But hitches and trailers are a different matter. Buyer Beware! At best it is extremely difficult, if not impossible, to purchase 'off the shelf' hitches and trailers. This paper will outline a design for hitches and trailers that has been tested and proven over many years to deliver good quality and trouble-free service. Anyone choosing to use either of the designs must make certain that the recommended specifications are followed exactly as to dimensions and quality of material used. Anything less can result in failure of the units, or less than desirable performance.

Tractors

The most common and essential piece of equipment used in labour-based road works as a prime mover is the agricultural tractor. In most cases the tractor fleet represents the largest single capital investment and entails the greatest costs

1

for operation and maintenance. Most of these costs are necessary and cannot be avoided. However, in many cases these costs are unnecessarily large due to insufficient care in procuring appropriate makes and models for the geographical area in which they are to be used. When procuring tractors for this type of work several factors must be considered.

What is available?
Very often labour-based road maintenance projects and programmes are funded externally and the funding agent will insist on providing equipment from home countries. This in itself has its merits, but does the host country have the back-up support to sustain this equipment once it arrives? We can train operators and mechanics and include 10–15 per cent spares with the initial order but what do we do in the long term when the spares stock diminishes? A more sensible solution is to use that type of equipment which is most common and available in the area, with a solid dealer back-up for spares and service. This will go a long way towards reducing maintenance costs and standardizing the fleet with as few makes and models as possible, which is essential to good fleet management.

What size?
Traditionally the 55–65 HP 2 WD agricultural tractor has been the first choice. The main reasons for this is that it is the most commonly available tractor in developing countries, it is fairly basic and simple to maintain, and the HP rating has been judged as adequate for hauling the standard three cubic metre gravel trailer over most terrain. There are a few exceptions to this, where a four-wheel drive or a higher horsepower may be desired due to severe conditions. When purchasing agricultural tractors in this HP range specifications would be limited to such options as two- or four-wheel drive, with or without hydraulics. To request buyer options for this size tractor, such as a heavier axle or different gearbox ratios would be highly impractical, if not impossible. However, two items that are available and which should be considered are industrial grade tyres together with front and rear weights.

Hitches
All agricultural tractors have the option of being supplied with or without a hitch. The hitches supplied from the factory are of the three point lift hitch or straight drawbar type designed specifically for attaching agricultural implements. All of these hitches work well for the purpose for which they were designed but they are unsuitable for use with the heavy gravel haulage trailers used in roadworks. The main reasons for this are:

○ Gravel trailers are hitched and unhitched many times a day.

○ Agricultural hitch pickup devices are too light for the drawbar weight of the gravel trailer.
○ Agricultural hitches do not allow for weight transfer to the tractor front axle.

To overcome these difficulties, a specially designed hitch has been developed for use with this tractor/trailer combination. This design allows for four-point attachment to the tractor and is easily adapted to most of the common tractors in use today. The hitch drawbar attachment is positioned forward of the rear axle allowing for a weight transfer from the trailer drawbar to the tractor front axle. This is essential to eliminate the tendency of the tractor to lift the front wheels off the ground when climbing steep inclines, such as are experienced in gravel pits. This is also a serious safety factor, as it improves traction for steering and it also eliminates the tendency of the tractor to turn over backwards on steep inclines. Although this redesigned hitch is approximately twice the price of the standard agricultural hitch, it virtually eliminates cases of complete hitch failure, whereas the standard hitch experiences these types of failures on a regular basis when being used under the severe conditions experienced in roadworks.

Design

The design of this hitch allows the tractor hydraulic system to be used in lowering, raising and locking the hitch drawbar without the operator leaving his seat. This is both a time-saving and safety factor. The locking system is entirely mechanical, thus avoiding any possibility of the trailer becoming detached from the tractor through hydraulic failure. The basic design although robust, is simple – allowing for ease of maintenance and replacement of worn parts using very basic workshop equipment.

Hitch/trailer link

The most common connecting link between the hitch and the trailer is a straight pin or hook which attaches directly to a towing eye welded to the trailer drawbar. This towing eye can be either of the solid fixed type or a swivel type allowing for rotational movement. Although the pin and eye link system is the cheapest coupling system to install, it does have one serious drawback originating in the slack between the pin and the eye. This slack is necessary to compensate for the twist factor between the tractor and the trailer. However, it also causes a shock factor – forward and backward movement – to the hitch mountings on the tractor. This is one of the primary causes of hitch failure. To overcome this it is strongly recommended that the coupling link be converted to a ball and socket system. This system completely eliminates the shock factor while still allowing for rotational and vertical movement between the tractor and trailer.

General descriptive line drawings for this hitch are provided in Figure 1.2 Specific dimensions are not indicated as these will differ according to the type and make of tractor application. Relevant material sizes are indicated where applicable, and these should not be altered in an effort to make the hitch lighter or cheaper.

Trailers

Of all the equipment used in labour-based road maintenance, the trailer has to be the most critical and controversial. Over the years many options have been tried with varying degrees of success. The most significant problems encountered with all types of trailer were poor structural design and the use of inadequate materials by manufactures. There are probably as many opinions as to what constitutes the ideal trailer as there are types of trailer. The one thing that is certain is that a suitable trailer for road gravelling works cannot be purchased 'off the shelf'. There are many companies that manufacture and supply light utility and agricultural trailers and these trailers are, as their name implies, light and utility. They will not withstand the constant heavy loads and daily use (or abuse) of road gravelling works. The most practical solution to this question is a trailer designed specifically for roadworks with a view to durability and simplicity. For the purposes of this paper we shall look at one such design that has been developed and used extensively in Kenya during the last six years.

Background

Over the years many different designs and types of trailers have been experimented with and used. Probably the most commonly used with tractors in the earlier years were hydraulic tipping trailers. These were usually made in the four cubic metre size. The two main problems were: first, the bodies were too light to support the load and the tipping attachment when lifting, and

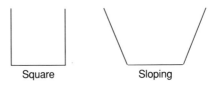

Figure 1.1 *The bucket design is either of the square side or sloping side type. The sloping sided trailer allows for easier unloading of material, especially when it is wet*

second, and more difficult to overcome, was the maintenance of the hydraulic system. This had proven to be very costly and time-consuming. Any time advantage gained in the rapid unloading was soon lost through downtime for maintenance. The end result for these trailers was the removal of the hydraulics and the welding together of the main frame and the lifting frame, converting them to a solid non-tipping trailer.

Trailers come with several options or combinations of unloading doors. Front doors, tail gates and side doors have all been used, either singly or in combinations, in an effort to shorten unloading time. Field trials have shown that at best the time saved by using doors is minimal, if not non-existent. The overall availability of this type of trailer over one without doors is much lower due to the periodic maintenance required to the doors.

Guidelines to trailer design

The design of a serviceable trailer requires consideration of certain points:

○ In most cases the trailer will be towed by light agricultural tractors and as a result the static weight of the trailer should not be greater than necessary. To 'over-spec.' the trailer is to 'over-burden' the tractor.

○ The trailer designed for labour-based work methods will be loaded by hand; therefore the trailer height should be kept as low as is practicable.

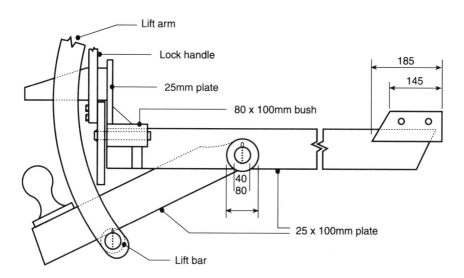

Figure 1.2 *Transfer hitch*

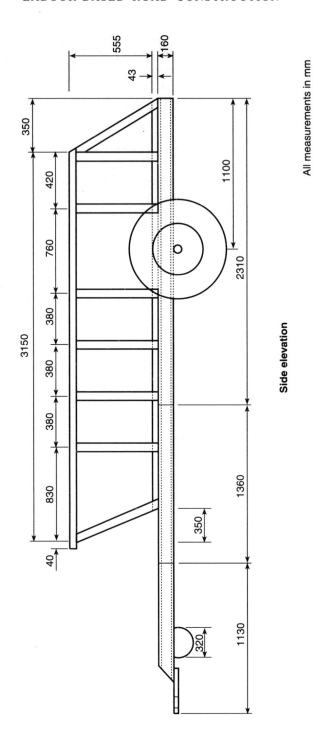

Figure 1.3 *Three cubic metre trailer*

○ The trailer should be robust enough to stand up to the rigours of roadworks but at the same time it should maintain a certain amount of flexibility to avoid cracking and breaking components.
○ The design should be such that the trailer can be easily reproduced in developing countries with minimal equipment and imported components.

General description
As mentioned earlier, for the purpose of this paper we are dealing only with the trailer that has been developed over the last few years in Kenya. This trailer incorporates features from some of the trailers mentioned above, and others through experience. The trailer is of the three cubic metre size with sloping sides and front panel. The rear of the bucket is left open. There are no doors or tail gate.

There are several key areas in the design of trailers to be considered and the most important of these is the frame. This is an area where manufacturers often go wrong when building a trailer for industrial use. The traditional box frame or unibody construction is fine for light or utility trailers, but consistently fails under the constant heavy use of roadworks. These faults show up in body distortion resulting in cracks and breakage of the drawbar. To overcome these faults the Kenya trailer has adopted a modified V shaped frame, eliminating drawbar breakage and body distortion. Sketches of this design can be seen in Figures 1.3 and 1.4.

Another key area of the trailer design is the construction of the bucket. Most manufactures use standard size sheets of metal which are not large enough, and which require additional pieces to be welded together resulting in many welded joints. The Kenya trailer uses only three pieces cut to length to cover the entire height and width of the trailer. This results in only two cross welds on the floor and sides of the bucket. The upper outside edge of the bucket is then reinforced with 40 × 40mm square tubing. This results in a stronger and more flexible bucket, preventing cracks and distortions. Sketches of these details can be seen in Figure 1.5.

A third key area that requires serious consideration is the axle. Rather then use a single beam, the Kenya trailer has an axle made from two U hot rolled steel channels 100 × 50 × 6mm welded back to back, with the stub axle welded in between. This provides for ease of manufacture and eliminates the necessity of having a special single beam casting of the axle to provide the necessary strength. A second critical factor concerning the axle is its attachment location on the chassis in relation to the load. This is very important for weight distribution to the tractor hitch. For this particular tractor/trailer combination the weight on the hitch should not exceed one-third of the loaded trailer weight. This weight distribution avoids overloading the tractor hydraulics and improves traction on both the front wheels (for more positive steering) and the rear wheels (to reduce slippage).

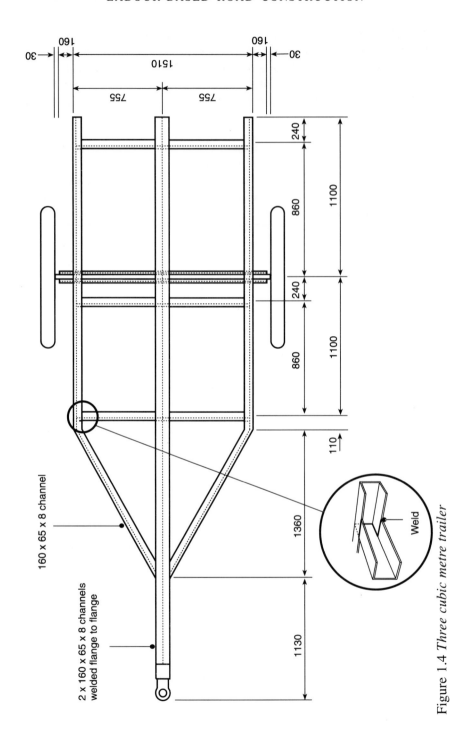

160 x 65 x 8 channel

2 x 160 x 65 x 8 channels
welded flange to flange

Weld

Figure 1.4 *Three cubic metre trailer*

Stub axle

This is the item on the trailer most likely to have to be imported. Very few foundries in developing countries have the capability to cast these units to the required metal composition standards. Failure to meet these standards will result in failure of the stub axle. The Kenya trailer uses an imported stub axle of 500 × 80 × 80mm with an individual load rating of 7000kg and a wheel mounting of 6 × 18mm studs. This gives a single stub axle rating equal to the total loaded weight of the trailer, which has proved to be more than adequate.

The tyres used on this axle are the standard 900 × 20 × 14 ply truck tyre.

Specifications

As stated earlier, one of the problems encountered in manufacturing trailers is poor structural design and the use of unsuitable material. The key factor in the procurement of trailers is that the supplier selected must be capable of delivering goods of high quality workmanship. Second, clear and concise

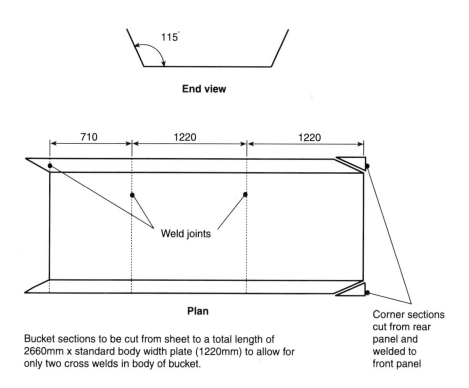

End view

Plan

Bucket sections to be cut from sheet to a total length of 2660mm x standard body width plate (1220mm) to allow for only two cross welds in body of bucket.

Corner sections cut from rear panel and welded to front panel

Figure 1.5 *Three cubic metre trailer (bucket configuration)*

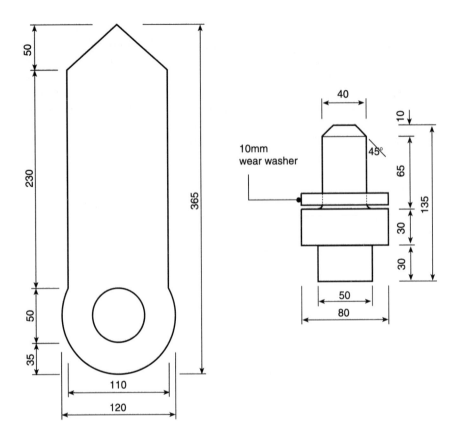

Figure 1.6 *Towing eye and pin assembly*

specifications should be supplied to manufactures. Third, during the manufacturing process there should be constant monitoring of the work in progress by the client's representative. During this monitoring special attention should be paid to such items as the quality of material, welds and adherence to specifications.

The following are the specifications for the Kenya trailer.

Technical specifications for 3 cubic metre trailer

Size
The trailer shall be 3 cubic metre capacity of the following dimensions:

Total height to top of body	1300mm
Total length	4800mm
Width	1570mm

Inside dimensions of bucket	
Top width	2000mm
Bottom width	1500mm
Length	3150mm
Depth	555mm

Body

The body of the trailer (bucket) shall be all steel plate of 3mm thickness reinforced by cold pressed steel channel of 40 × 80 × 3mm at intervals as shown in Figure 1.5.

Axle

Shall be made of two U hot rolled steel channels of 100 × 50 × 6mm. Welded together with a stub axle welded between them. There shall be a distance of 100mm between the wheel and the body. Total length of the channels 1860mm.

The axle shall be located 1100mm from the back of the chassis.

Chassis

The middle member of the chassis shall be of two U channels of 160 × 65 × 8mm welded together to form the drawbar of 1130mm in length as shown in Figure 1.4. Side and cross members of the chassis shall be of U channels of 160 × 65 × 8mm.

Details

Stub axle:

Axle Stub	80 × 80mm
Axle length	500mm
Axle rated load	7000kg

Wheels:

Un-braked, 6 studs

Tyre size	900 × 20, 14 ply
Stud size	18mm
Centre circle	161mm
Bolt circle	205mm
Thread pitch	1.5mm

Towing eyes:
  To be cut from 32mm steel plate as in Figure 1.6.
  Optional: 80mm ball and socket

Rims:
  7.0 - 20 with lock ring

Painting:
  One primer coat
  Two coats industrial grade paint.

CHAPTER 2

Intermediate equipment for labour-based roadworks

B. Hancox

This paper addresses the subject of intermediate equipment and presents a concise review of two items of 'state of the art' equipment designed and manufactured in Kenya. These items are a tractor towing hitch and a three cubic metre gravel trailer, both designed and developed in response to the failure of European designs to withstand the severe operating conditions found on labour-based road projects.

The paper first analyses the Kenyan towing hitch by discussing its design and suggesting possible modifications, while at the same time comparing the hitch with 'state of the art' European designs based on British and ISO standard dimensions. Current material selection is also discussed, together with an outline of the EU's directive on the fatigue testing and certification scheme for tractor towing hitches. Attention is drawn to the need for selected towing hitches and trailer hitch rings to be fatigue tested and monitored for wear under operational conditions, so that the information can be made available to interested parties.

Kenya's 3m³ trailer is discussed in the light of its development from a 1987 prototype and the features that have been adopted. The paper also offers suggestions on how to lower the loading height by 200mm simply by rearranging the chassis layout.

Tractor-mounted towing hitches

The wear and breakage of tractor towing hitches has always been a topic of conversation, and to the uninitiated engineer the ball joint coupling offers the best solution. (See Figure 2.1.) However, when you consider that one tractor serves two trailers during gravel haulage, then the ball joint becomes impractical, not only because of the time taken to switch from one trailer to another, but the ball and cup are both machined components and require greasing. Given the dusty conditions of a borrow pit, the grease would soon form an

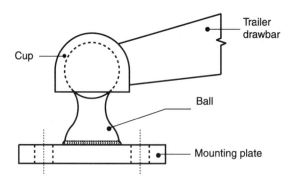

Figure 2.1 *Ball joint coupling*

effective grinding paste. The author would strongly argue that the existing method of hitching trailers to tractors, using a towing hook and hitch ring, remains the most appropriate, sustainable and cost-effective solution for labour-based road construction.

The towing hitch specified for use by the Kenyan Ministry of Works is sketched in sectional view in Figure 2.2. The whole assembly is manufactured using mild steel plate and joined using electric arc welding. This process produces a strong fabrication and because of the wide tolerances between moving parts, the assembly is easily manufactured by local workshops in Nairobi. However, there are inherent design problems associated with the hitch which have been identified through operational experience, and these are as follows:

○ rapid wear of the towing hook and trailer hitch ring
○ the security of the towing hook mounting frame is difficult to maintain
○ it is necessity to remove the PTO shaft from the tractor before fitting the mounting frame
○ the design of the mounting frame is not easily transferable to other makes of tractor.

Taking each of these factors in turn, design problems are discussed and solutions suggested that may be of value to other users and interested parties.

Towing hook and trailer hitch ring wear
Rapid wear of the towing hook can be attributed to two main causes; one is the incorrect profile of the towing hook in relation to the trailer hitch ring, and the second is the material used in manufacture. From the sketch in Figure 2.3, it can be seen that wear between the towing pin and base plate and the trailer's hitch ring will be accelerated. This is due to the excessive point loads caused

14

by the very small bearing surfaces available between the trailer hitch ring and the edges of the base plate, as well as at the normal points of contact between trailer hitch ring and towing pin. These point loads generate high frictional forces which are the cause of the accelerated metal-to-metal wear.

The normal patterns of wear on the towing pin and base plate are shown in Figure 2.3 and although one of the main reasons for this accelerated wear is the poor profile of these two components, which results in excessive play between towing pin and the trailer hitch ring, there is also another major contributory factor – the hardness of the material being used for the towing pin and base plate.

To overcome the profile problem, a British Standard (6108) (subsequently ISO standard 6489) was developed that specifies the dimensional requirements for a hook-type coupling on agricultural towing vehicles. (See Figure

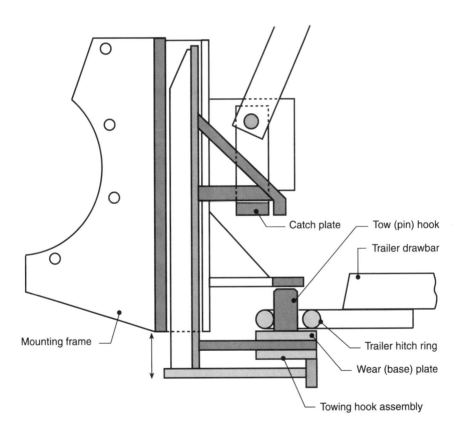

Figure 2.2 *Towing hitch – Kenya ministry of public works*

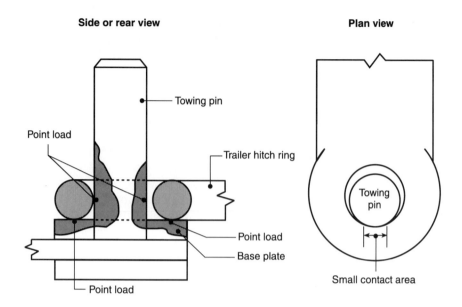

Figure 2.3 *Kenya towing hitch wear – three planes of motion*

2.4). This standard also allows for the mechanical connection with towed trailers fitted with a hitch ring manufactured to ISO standard 5692. (See Figure 2.5). Both standards, for the hook-type coupling and trailer hitch ring, provide recommended dimensions only and do not provide material specifications.

From the specifications given in Figure 2.4, it is clear that the standard provides for a maximum contact area to be maintained between the mating surfaces of the tractor towing hook and the trailer hitch ring, and that contact is always on a radial surface in the three planes of tractor/trailer motion, i.e. yaw, pitch and roll. This arrangement avoids the point loads between components that are present in the Kenyan design. This radial contact can be seen in Figure 2.6 and demonstrates that by adopting an appropriate profile for both the towing hook and the trailer hitch ring, maximum contact area will be maintained. This will keep frictional forces to a minimum and reduce the rate of wear, even when using mild steel, as in the case of the Kenyan design.

It is relatively easy to produce the complicated profile specified in the standards using drop forging techniques, but to manufacture them in basic workshops is impractical. One suggestion is to use the category one steel balls used in the lower lift arms of the tractor's three point linkage system. Using these two balls at right angles to each other, as shown in Figure 2.7, will provide a profile similar to the ISO standard 6489. The contact surfaces have been case hardened, making them hard wearing and capable of withstanding shock loads. The overall dimensions do not conform to the ISO standard but they are closer than the present Kenyan design and all contact mating surfaces will be acting on a radius, which will reduce wear considerably. This modification can easily be incorporated into the existing design, and the steel balls are available from any tractor dealership as a stock item.

The second cause of rapid towing hook and trailer hitch ring wear is the specification of the material used. In the Kenyan design, the towing hook, which is made up of the towing pin and base plate, is made from mild steel which is cheap, readily available and easy to weld and machine. From Table 2.1 it can be seen that as the specification moves from mild steel through to a high carbon/alloy steel, the wear resistance improves considerably, as measured by its Brinell hardness number. The disadvantage is that the weldability gets more difficult and the cost increases due to the addition of alloys and the heat treatment necessary to maintain acceptable strength and fatigue properties for this application.

The major European manufacturers have adopted an EN 19 steel specification for their towing hooks. This steel, which can be drop forged to the ISO

Table 2.1: Common steel alloys used for drop forged towing hooks and trailer hitch rings

Class	British Standards Number	Category	Use	Tensile strength N/mm^2	Weldability	Brinell hardness number
070M26		Mild steel	Hitch ring	695	No preheat	165
	4360 EN43A	Structural steel	Hitch ring	695	No preheat	201/255
	4360 EN50B	Structural steel	Hitch ring	695	No preheat	201/255
080M40	EN 8	Medium carbon steel	Hitch ring	695	No preheat	201/255
605M30	EN 16	High carbon / alloy steel	Hitch ring	927	Preheat + slow cooling	293/352
605M36	EN 16D	High carbon / alloy steel	Hitch ring	927	Preheat + slow cooling	293/352
709M40	EN 19	High carbon / alloy steel	Tow hook	1004	Preheat + slow cooling	321/363

6489 specification and hardened to Brinell hardness number 363, gives excellent wear properties plus a high fatigue strength. All European-manufactured towing hitches must now be tested and certified under an EU directive number 89/173. This directive states that mechanical couplings between tractors and towed vehicles, and the vertical load on the coupling point, must be subjected to a statutory dynamic or static load test prior to certification. Nevertheless, this test only measures the fatigue strength of a towing hook and does not indicate the wear resistance of the material used in its manufacture.

Prior to this directive coming into force, UK manufacturers had recognized that towing hooks manufactured to the existing ISO standard specifications were liable to premature failure through excessive wear when used on constant trailer work. One manufacturer produces a non-standard hook which

BS 6108: Part 1: 1993 Couplings on agricultural towing vehicles Part 1 – Hook type
ISO 6489 – 1: 1991 Agricultural vehicles – Mechanical connection on towing vehicle Part 1: Hook type.

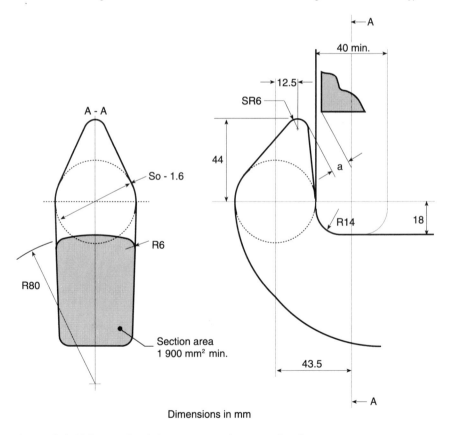

Dimensions in mm

Figure 2.4 *ISO standard dimensions of towing hook*

BS 5891:1980 Ring type hitch on agricultural trailers and implements.
ISO 5692 : 1979 Agricultural vehicles - mechanical connections on towed vehicles - hitch rings

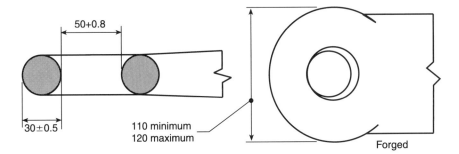

Figure 2.5 *ISO standard dimension for trailer hitch ring*

has a greater cross-sectional area than the minimum $1900 \, mm^2$ specified in the ISO standard.

It would be of great benefit to the labour-based roads sector if field trials could be undertaken using an ISO standard and a non-standard towing hook, and actual rates of wear monitored over a two-year period. Such information would enable a standard specification to be drawn up for procurement purposes, and also provide the necessary evidence if a change to the ISO standard was found necessary.

Trailer hitch rings are also a major wear item and their dimensions are also subjected to ISO 5692 standard, as shown in Figure 2.5. Again, this standard only provides dimensions and gives no guidance on material selection, which has a significant influence on the rate of wear. All European-manufactured trailer hitch rings conform to the main ISO standard dimensions, but manufacturers have again recognized that wear is the major problem for trailer hitch rings as well as for tow hitches. Consequently, they provide a range of material options and also two sizes of material thickness (30 and 40mm) in an effort to extend the life of these components.

The main materials on offer for trailer hitch rings are given in Table 2.1, and they range from mild steel through to the high carbon alloy steels which give excellent wear properties. As mentioned earlier, weldability becomes a problem with the high carbon alloys and the component requires pre-heating prior to welding and slow cooling after welding. Cost is also a major factor, and one manufacturer has responded again by producing a trailer hitch ring, using a relatively cheap medium carbon steel with an average rate of wear, but because

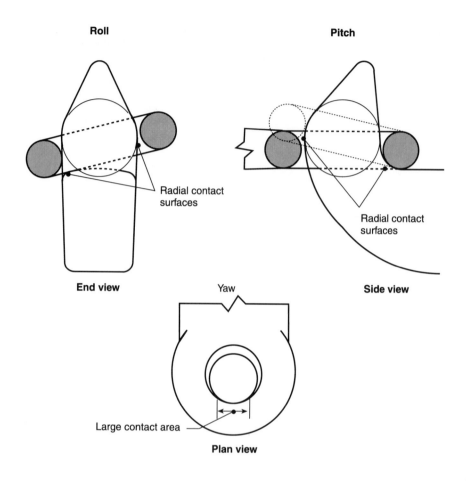

Figure 2.6 *ISO standard towing hook – three planes of motion*

of a larger material thickness (40mm) than specified under the ISO standard, the wear rate is equivalent to the more expensive alloy steels using a standard thickness. It should be noted that it is usual practice for towing hitch material to be harder than for the trailer hitch ring, as it is cheaper to replace the trailer hitch ring when it wears out.

In order to develop a standard specification for procurement purposes, selected hitch rings of differing thickness and material specifications need to be tested together with locally manufactured towing hooks, under field conditions, and the rates of wear monitored. One manufacturer is already willing to assist in providing samples for field trials.

Security of mounting frame

The second major problem to be experienced with the Kenyan-designed hitch is in maintaining the security of the mounting frame which attaches the towing hook to the tractor. The original six (16mm diameter) bolts fastening the frame to the tractor's rear transmission housing constantly worked loose, resulting in stripped threads, chipped casting and sheared bolts. A previous recommendation was to weld side plates on to the back of the mounting plate and make use of the pre-drilled and tapped bolt holes on the side of the transmission housing. This modification has been incorporated into the design currently used by the Kenyans on their International 733 tractor, but there has been no feedback on how successful this modification has been.

Referring again to the EEC directive on the testing of couplings between tractors and towed vehicles, the dynamic loading of the towing hook undertaken during the test measures not only the fatigue strength of the towing hook but also that of the mounting frame that attaches the hook to the tractor. Horizontal and vertical forces acting on the towing hook are calculated to a specified formula which takes into account the weight of the tractor and the weight of the trailer, as specified by the manufacturer. These two component

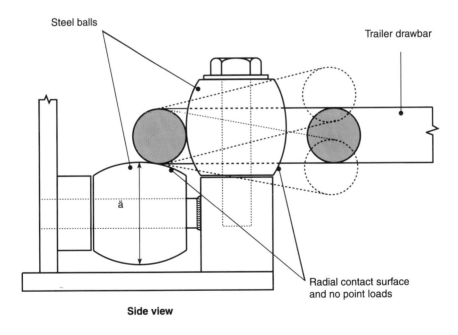

Figure 2.7 *Kenyan towing hook modification using steel balls*

Table 2.2: Towing hook mounting brackets under bending moments and torsion

Bolt	Vertical load		Horizontal stress		Total stress	
	Shear stress kN/m^2	Tensile stress kN/m^2	Shear stress kN/m^2	Tensile stress kN/m^2	Shear stress kN/m^2	Tensile stress kN/m^2
A1	–	14.6	–	113.3	–	128
A2	–	16.4	–	66.0	–	82
A3	–	17.7	–	18.7	–	36
A4	35.0	–	17.5	–	17.5	–
A5	37.5	–	19.0	–	18.5	–
A6	38.5	–	21.0	–	17.5	–
A7	42.5	–	21.5	–	21.0	–

forces are combined into a single resultant force which is reproduced on the test rig to load the towing hook and mounting frame for two million load cycles at a speed of five cycles per second. The whole test takes approximately 222 hours to complete, and on completion both the towing hook and mounting frame are subjected to a tear test using colour penetration or similar techniques. If no fractures are detected in the mounting bolts, frame or hook, and the mounting bolts have stayed secure, then a certificate is issued by the testing station. In the UK this is at Silsoe Research Institute.

This test is very effective in quickly identifying poor design, inadequate material selection and bolt security. Although it would prove costly to offer the Kenyan design for testing, nevertheless this certification requirement for towing hitches and mounting frames should be standard procedure in the procurement of towing hitches for use on labour-based road projects. Even locally-made hitches, such as the Kenyan one, should be subjected to at least a static load test, as recommended by the EU directive.

In the absence of any opportunity to submit the Kenyan hitch to such a load test, and in order to assess bolt security on the redesigned towing hitch when in service, the stresses in each bolt due to bending moments, shear forces and torsion have been calculated under static load conditions . The horizontal and vertical force components were calculated using the EU test procedures. The results of the calculations are given in Table 2.2 and show that the maximum stress values of each bolt is significantly lower than the maximum tensile stress of 221.7 MN/m^2 for an M16 high tensile bolt.

These low stress values indicate that even though the actual forces acting on the mounting bolts in service will be dynamic, this shock loading will not produce a resultant force on any one bolt sufficient to cause the bolt to break. However, from the figures in Table 2.2, the shear stresses in bolts A4, A5, A6 and A7 have been created by two torsional forces acting in a clockwise and anti-clockwise direction. These two forces comprise of the weight of the trailer acting vertically downwards on the towing hook and then transmitted to the load-carrying latch, plus the horizontal force acting on the towing hook caused by the rolling resistance of the trailer, and grade resistance. These two forces and the resultant bending moment and torsional forces acting on the bolted system are shown in Figure 2.8.

The shear forces calculated in bolts A4, A5, A6 and A7 act in both positive (clockwise) and negative (anti-clockwise) directions, and in a static constant load situation the resultant shear forces are in a positive direction as indicated in Table 2.2. However, in a dynamic situation when the towing hook and

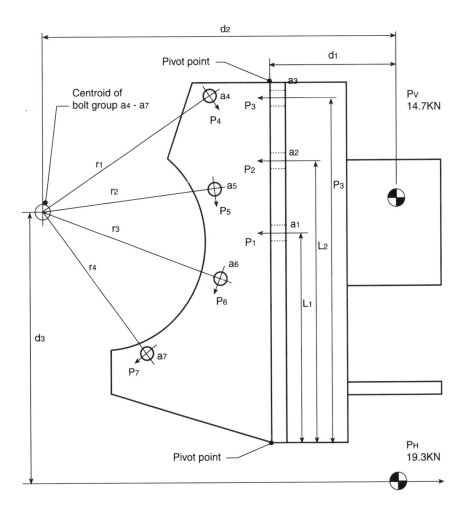

Figure 2.8 *Kenyan towing hitch – bolted system*

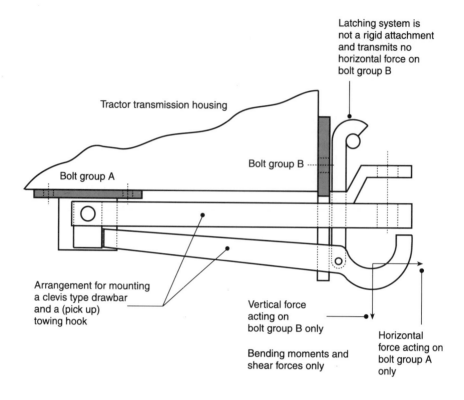

Latching system is
not a rigid attachment
and transmits no
horizontal force on
bolt group B

Tractor transmission housing

Bolt group B

Bolt group A

Arrangement for mounting
a clevis type drawbar
and a (pick up)
towing hook

Vertical force
acting on
bolt group B only

Horizontal
force acting on
bolt group A
only

Bending moments and
shear forces only

Figure 2.9 *Redesign of Kenyan towing hitch*

mounting bracket are subjected to shock loads, such as a bouncing trailer and
tractor, these shear forces will not only change in magnitude but their resultant
forces will constantly change direction. Under these intermittent and oscillating forces, bolts A4 to A7 are unlikely to shear off, but they will undoubtedly
work loose, causing the mounting frame to move. Once sufficient movement
has been created, the bolts will work themselves loose because it is only the
frictional forces between the bolt heads and mounting plate that will be
resisting this movement.

In order to assist these frictional forces and help to prevent movement, the
manufacturing quality of the mounting frame has to be improved as follows:

○ Bolt holes must be drilled in the mounting frame with the correct clearance
for the bolt size in use.
○ The bolt holes in the mounting frame must align accurately with the pre-
drilled and tapped holes in the tractor's transmission casing to prevent the
need to widen the hole during fitting.

○ The mounting bolts need to be of a fine-pitch thread as these tend not to loosen as easily as a coarse-pitch thread. Also, a fine-pitch thread has a greater stress area than a coarse-pitch, and tends to have a greater load carrying capability when correctly selected.

However, the tapped holes in the transmission housing are coarse pitch threads.

My conclusions after assessing Kenya's towing hitch are as follows: The intermittent and oscillating nature of the forces acting on the towing hitch will always result in bolts working loose, even if the correct bolt hole clearances are provided and there is accurate alignment of all bolt holes and the correct specification of bolts are used. Therefore, the mounting frame and towing hook, i.e. towing pin and base plate, need to be redesigned so that the vertical and horizontal forces acting on the towing hook are carried at two separately bolted mounting points, as indicated in Figure 2.9. The benefits of adopting this design are as follows:

○ The vertical and horizontal forces acting on each bolt group will be independent of each other and consist of bending moment and shear forces only.
○ Stress calculations will be simplified and manufacturing accuracy will not be so critical.
○ There will be no need to remove the PTO shaft prior to fitting the towing hitch to the tractor.
○ The added flexibility of having two mounting points will enable the new hitch to be fitted to most makes of tractor without major modifications to the drawings.

Although the Kenyan towing hitch is both appropriate and repairable, it still has the major design problems which have been identified in this paper, and they still need to be resolved. There are also questions that need to be asked about the European-designed towing hitches and why they have failed; also, which components failed and what caused them to fail. Answers to these questions would enable modifications to be developed in co-operation with the relevant manufacturers, or an appropriate local design to be developed.

Local designs must be encouraged and developed, as with the Kenyan design, along the lines already suggested. Fatigue and wear testing and monitoring need also to be implemented, as it is only by testing and comparing the performance of both European and local designs and materials, that reliable recommendations and specifications can be made available.

Three cubic metre gravel trailer

The second item of 'state of the art' equipment from Kenya is the 3m³ gravel trailer. This trailer was originally designed as a 4m³ trailer until field trials

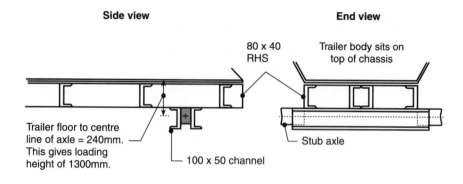

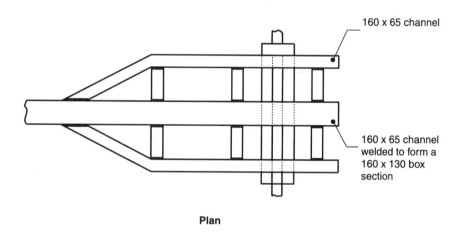

Figure 2.10 *Kenyan 3m³ gravel trailer – chassis design*

found that, because of the length of the trailer, it was taking too long to unload even though it was fitted with top hinged doors at the front which allowed the trailer to be unload at both front and rear at the same time. One feature from the 4m³ trailer that has been adopted is the use of 900 × 20 truck tyres. This size of tyre is common in Kenya and is readily available, which is an important consideration when procuring or designing intermediate equipment for labour-based road construction. The down side to using these tyres is the absence of tyre wall flexibility and a lack of cushioning which is common with normal trailer tyres, as they are designed for un-sprung applications but are not readily available overseas. Therefore, as a consequence of using the 900 × 20 tyres, the shock loading on the axles increases and axle load ratings must be revised upwards to compensate. On the Kenyan trailer, the distributed weight on one wheel when fully loaded is approximately 2.25 tonnes and the stub axles rating selected is 7 tonnes.

The sloping tail section of the trailer body has also been retained. This feature was incorporated into the original 4m³ trailer design because the old tipping trailers used in Kenya were originally supplied with tail gates. These had long since been thrown away but the trailers were still being used, as very little material was lost from the back once the gravel in the trailer had reached its natural angle of repose. As the tail gates were discarded the side boards were now unsupported at the rear and were subjected to a constant vibration due to travel over rough ground. The resulting stress set up in the each side board caused fatigue fracture. The whole rear corner section broke off, roughly at an angle corresponding to the angle of repose of the gravel being carried. This new profile was introduced as a permanent feature as it offered both a cost and weight saving.

In the original 4m³ trailer design, the loading height, which is critical for a hand loading trailer, was kept to a maximum of 1100mm. However, with the present design the loading height has been increased to 1300mm. This height can be reduced by 200mm if the original 4m³ trailer chassis design is adopted, but instead of using the monocoque construction method, the existing chassis can be rearranged so that the axle can be dropped 200mm, as shown in Figures 2.10 and 2.11. The new chassis layout does not call for a radical change in design, as it uses the same number of steel sections, and the welds are in approximately the same areas. The stress distribution should therefore be unchanged.

As trailer loading height is a major factor in designing a hand-loaded trailer, it is suggested that a scale model chassis could be constructed of both the existing Kenyan design and also the proposed redesign shown in Figure 2.11. These models could then be load-tested for weld and structural strength, simply by using a hydraulic press.

The Kenyan design does not have top hinged unloading doors at the front of the trailer. These doors are supposed to enable a trailer to be unloaded faster than just rear unloading because material is shovelled only half the distance. Although the structural strength of the trailer is not compromised by the provision of these doors, they do increase the price of the trailer and there may be operational problems, such as doors becoming bent and catches being broken. In the absence of any feedback from the Kenyans on why the doors were dropped from their design, one can only speculate that the additional cost, and the operational problems experienced, outweighed the benefits of saving a few minutes of unloading time.

To conclude this section, the Kenyans have based their present design on a 4m³ trailer which was first constructed in 1987 and has been tried and tested under operational conditions. From the trial results, their present 3m³ trailer was designed incorporating the best features of the 4m³ trailer. This approach has been a slow but excellent way of developing intermediate equipment which is appropriate for the countries where labour-based construction is practised, and ensures the equipment can be easily maintained and repaired in those countries.

This approach should be adopted for the development of all intermediate equipment to enable the most appropriate and reliable designs to be achieved. In terms of the present trailer, design work should continue to reduce the loading height as suggested and scale models used for chassis testing purposes, prior to the building of a full size trailer.

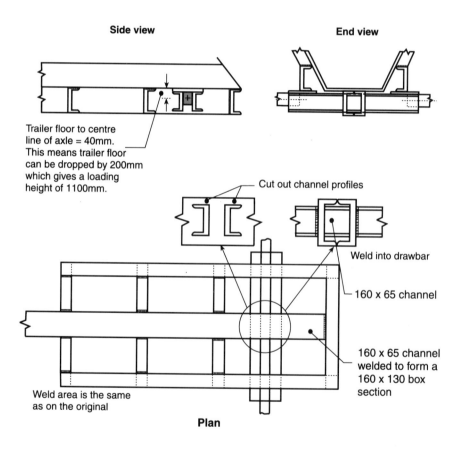

Figure 2.11 *Kenyan 3m³ gravel trailer – chassis redesign to lower loading height*

Conclusions

This paper has concentrated on two important items of intermediate equipment, the towing hitch and the gravel trailer. Both items have been developed locally in Kenya in response to a need for appropriate equipment after it became apparent that equipment designed for European conditions was inappropriate for the operational conditions found on labour-based projects.

However, even when considering just these two items, it becomes clear that a co-ordinated effort needs to be undertaken first, to catalogue the designs of towing hitches and trailers in current use on labour-based road projects. The second stage is to study each design and identify component failures to determine whether they are due to design, material or operational failures. Third, select the most appropriate designs through working with local and international manufacturers, end users and international standards committees. Finally, develop these designs through rigorous testing, to produce appropriate specifications and drawings that are reliable and can be used either for international procurement or for local manufacturing. This will also prevent repeated failures of equipment on projects throughout the world, and continuing attempts to reinvent the wheel.

The multilateral and bilateral agencies have a role to play, by adopting a co-ordinating role and providing the necessary funding to undertake the basic research and development required to develop reliable specifications. They should then enforce the use of standard specifications and drawings in the procurement or manufacture of intermediate equipment for all labour-based construction projects.

CHAPTER 3

Management of appropriate road technology in India

A. Murty

Introduction

Recognizing the urgent need for the generation of more employment in rural areas through socio-economic development programmes, the Indian Government has placed great emphasis on the development of rural roads. In India more than 54 per cent of villages are still to be provided with an all-weather road facility. This requires a huge quantity of funds and the optimum utilization of locally-available resources. There is therefore a need to develop appropriate and cost-effective technologies for constructing roads in rural areas.

Labour-intensive technologies

Rural roads are generally constructed by manual methods, employing local labourers using locally available hand-tools, equipment and materials. This sector has a considerable potential for employing the unskilled and semi-skilled labourers that are available in rural areas. These labourers normally possess their own rudimentary handtools and equipment for agricultural, road construction and repair activities.

Some of the commonly used handtools and equipment in road construction works are described in the Table 3.1.

Intermediate equipment

Keeping in mind the importance of providing employment opportunities in rural areas but at the same time ensuring a minimum standard of quality of roadworks, it is imperative to adopt an intermediate technology for road construction and maintenance. This technology would call for the use of agricultural equipment such as a tractor-towed plough disc-harrow, rotavator/rotifer, water sprinkler and light-weight road roller. The Central Road Research Institute (CRRI), New Delhi, has been undertaking research and development work to identify some of the tractor-towed equipment that may be used for different road construction activities. Field studies have been conducted to determine the efficiency of equipment in various operating conditions. It has also been found that wherever tractors and tractor-towed equipment are available, they can be hired for use in rural areas to achieve economy and quality work in road construction.

Description of intermediate equipment
Various operations can be carried out using tractors or animal-drawn equipment, which are described below:

Tiller/cultivator
○ A small tractor-towed agricultural implement useful for loosening the hard top surface prior to hand excavation.
○ Working speed 2km/hr
○ Working width 2m
○ Min. tractor power required 25hp

Table 3.1: Handtools and intermediate equipment used for various road construction activities

Type of operation	Handtools used	Equipment used (tractor towed)
Site clearance	Spade, shovel, digging fork, bill-hook, pick axes, wire/coir brushes and brooms	Dozer
Excavation	Spade, shovel	Tiller/cultivator, mould board plough and disc plough
Mixing	Spade	Rotivator
Pulverization	Spade, shovels	Disc harrow
Spreading soil/aggregates	Basket spreader	Grader / dozer
Watering	Animal-drawn water bowsers	Tractor towed water tank
Camber formation	Camber board, templates, shovel, spades and rakes	Grader, dozer
Compaction	Animal-drawn rollers, hand rammers	Tractor-towed rollers
Bitumen surface dressing	Drum kettle, perforated can and manually–operated sprayers wheelbarrows, rakes and spades	

Disc plough
○ An extremely useful implement for digging sand, clay, loam, black cotton soil and loose murrum.
○ Working speed 1.5 – 2.5km/hr
○ Three inclined blades 650mm diameter, 500mm apart
○ Min. tractor power required 35hp

Scraper
○ A digging and carrying device that picks up its own load through scraping the ground, and discharges by spreading the load.
○ Struck capacity 1m³
○ Min. tractor power required 45hp

Offset disc harrow
○ An implement used for pulverization and breaking up large soil clods. It consists of 500mm diameter saucer-shaped discs with sharpened edges arranged in two gangs, at 30° to each other.
○ Working width approximately 1.6m
○ Min. tractor power required 35hp

Rotavator
○ Equipment used for mixing soils with additives. It has L-shaped blades with sharpened edges. The blades are fitted around an axle which is rotated by a locking device fitted to the tractor.
○ Working width 1.25m
○ Working speed 2 – 3km/hr
○ Min. tractor power required 35 - 45hp

Grader plate
○ A tool used for levelling, scraping, grading and spreading soil or gravel for sub-bases. Used in conjunction with a scarifier, hard surfaces can be loosened and reshaped with the grader blade.
○ Blades can be pitched forward or back and tilted 15° to 30° left or right.
○ Grader can be reversed for backfilling.
○ Working width 1.8m
○ Min. tractor power required 35hp

Hydrodozer plate
○ A plate fitted to the front of a tractor used for cutting earth, moving material short distances and removing of small tree stumps.
○ Blade size 615mm × 2290mm
○ Blade cutting edge 140mm × 2285mm
○ Weight of hydrodozer attachment 850kg.

○ Recommended maximum tractor speeds
  blade raised 10 – 15km/hr
  blade lowered in operation 6km/hr

Animal drawn equipment
○ Concrete dead-weight roller
○ Steel drum dead-weight roller (CRRI Design 1)
○ Steel drum dead-weight roller with provision for additional ballast (CRRI
  Design 2)
○ Water bowsers
○ Bitumen boiler

The Indian Roads Congress has also published two small booklets related to the use of tools and equipment in concrete road and bituminous road construction, they are:

○ IRC : 43-1972. Recommended practices for tools, equipment and appliances for concrete road construction.
○ IRC : 72-1978. Recommended practice for use and upkeep of equipment, tools and appliances for bituminous pavement construction.

Small-scale contractor development in construction of secondary roads

Construction work in India is mostly executed by contractors on the basis of open competitive or negotiated tendering. The type of contracting employed varies from one place to another, different organizations following different systems for various types of contracts for the same type of work. Generally, for large projects the procedures followed are similar to those followed internationally. For the construction of secondary roads there are no well defined procedures for tendering.

In most cases, once a large contractor is awarded a project, he will lease out various components of work to smaller contractors for execution. Often the role of small contractors is to supply labourers, materials, etc. These small contractors, with little experience and expertise in the technical aspects of road building, and lack of skilled labour, equipment, etc., are unable to carry out the construction of secondary roads on their own.

It is important that the capacity level of small-scale contractors should be increased in technical aspects such as the use of handtools and intermediate equipment, optimal mix of labour and intermediate equipment and quality control for better construction. Training programmes on the above aspects should be arranged for the small contractors. Manuals and guidelines on the use of handtools, intermediate equipment, and quality control should also be prepared for use by these contractors. Use of local materials in construction work will result in development of the region by economizing on the cost of construction and maintenance. Some obvious advantages of employing small contractors are:

○ generation of more employment for the local population
○ development of technical skills within the rural workforce.

The disadvantages are:

○ a very close supervisory input is required to ensure the quality of construction
○ time delays and escalation of costs can occur due to non-availability of manpower during agricultural seasons.

The advantages and disadvantages of employing small contractors for the construction of secondary roads indicates a need to improve the tendering system and ensure that procedures are strictly followed. This will ensure that the roads constructed by small-scale contractors are durable and more economical, and that skilled manpower is trained for development of the region.

Institutional and organizational aspects

In India, rural roads are invariably constructed by several Governmental agencies, such as State Public Works Departments (PWD) and district/sub-district development authorities. They are funded through government-sponsored rural development programmes and development plans. These agencies prepare the various activities of rural road schemes individually and execute the work through contractors, or departmentally.

There is no centralized organization with the necessary internal structure to manage the construction and maintenance of rural roads. The availability of technically-trained manpower is also inadequate, as those employed in the rural road sector often do not remain within the sector due to lack of motivation and unattractive remuneration.

The most appropriate organization to manage rural roads would be a separate branch within the existing road construction authority. This organization would provide a channel for the allocation of funds exclusively for rural roads and permit the development of new methods for planning, design, construction and maintenance. It would also facilitate the appointment of small contractors for various types of work. A typical set-up proposed for rural road authority is given in Figures 3.1 and 3.2.

The responsibilities of the Rural Road Authority should include the provision of co-ordination between the various agencies involved in rural road development, evolving national guidelines and policies, mobilization of resources from various developmental programmes, drafting appropriate design criteria, labour-based and intermediate construction methods, quality

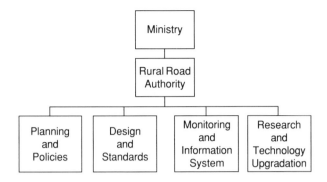

Figure 3.1 *Organization chart for rural roads authority at national level*

control, guiding research, promoting technology upgradation and technology transfer.

The authority should identify the training needs of its own staff at the working level by considering their job requirements and qualifications involved in rural road works. These training programmes should be co-ordinated through a centralized research and development organization and offered to the small contracting agencies.

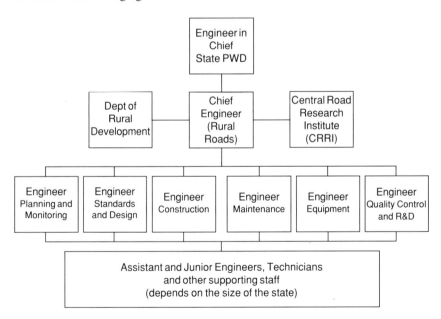

Figure 3.2 *Suggested organizational set-up at state level*

Conclusion

While developing appropriate technologies for construction of rural roads, a balanced approach should be adopted for a judicious blend of handtools, equipment and labour to suit and fit the overall concept of planning and construction of rural roads to achieve optimal use of resources and quality work. Suitable opportunities should be created for participatory programmes in rural roadworks by development of appropriate construction management techniques. Strengthening and reorganization of the management structure involved in rural roadworks is essential for the implementation of appropriate technologies.

References

1. Central Road Research Institute, Document on Development of Rural Roads in India, CRRI, New Delhi
2. Bureau of Indian Standards, Handbook of Agricultural Machinery Terminology, BIS, New Delhi
3. CRRI, Report on Tractor Bound Technologies for Rural Road Construction, 1990
4. CRRI, National Workshop on Rural Roads,
5. Ministry of Surface Transport (GOI), Asian Development Bank, Contractors manual for Management of Road Construction Project, prepared by Acer Freeman Fox in association with Taylor Woodrow International, Coopers & Lybrand and Stup Consultants Ltd, 1992
6. IRC: 43-1972 Recommended practice for tools, equipment and appliance for concrete road construction
7. IRC: 72-1978 Recommended practice for use and upkeep of equipment, tools and appliance for bituminous pavement construction.

CHAPTER 4

Equipment selection for rural road maintenance in developing countries

M. Hodge

For some considerable time now, a generation in fact, developing countries – especially African ones – have been struggling to move even a few steps towards an improved and sustainable infrastructure, particularly in the more rural areas. Without this, life is very difficult. Travel is difficult, for both social and business purposes. Produce cannot be easily taken to market and goods purchased at the market cannot easily be taken home to the village. Poor roads, if there at all, contribute to breakage and damage of both the vehicle carrying the produce, and often the produce itself, increasing the cost to the purchaser. Enormous amounts of time are wasted. In many cases a little maintenance would go a long way.

It has generally been the policy of large donor organizations to spend huge sums of money to prop up a very shaky structure. Rather than tackle the root of the problem, large, expensive and very visible equipment is paid for by the donor, who then leaves the local management to 'get on with it'. Unfortunately, in far too many cases the equipment is supplied without either technical or financial backing. After the initial honeymoon period when the new machine is all glossy and in full working order, a small and often simple component failure, probably due to contamination in the field, causes the machine to be abandoned while sufficient funds are found to purchase the part (if it is available locally), or a further delay is caused while the part is imported at even greater expense. During this period the work stops completely and the expensive glossy machine becomes another dinosaur parked in the bush!

It is apparent that a sustainable resource of some sort has to be provided to the local council or whoever is charged with the maintenance of the rural roads infrastructure, to allow the quality of life to improve in rural areas. Ideally this resource should based around the following parameters:

○ It should offer good value for money.
○ It should preferably be manufactured or assembled locally.

○ It should be easy and cheap to maintain.
○ It should have a remote, removable, readily available power source.
○ It should be used alongside, and in conjunction with, local labour.

While there is no doubt that large, high capital cost plant is required for the construction of roadways, especially if traffic levels are high, there is also the need for simple, cheap and easy-to-operate equipment for the maintenance and repair of the smaller, less heavily used roads and feeder roads. If the latter encourages the use of readily-available and cheap local labour and contractors, so much the better.

Simba International Ltd has been manufacturing and designing simple, robust and easy-to-maintain equipment for the agricultural and light civil engineering sector for some 20 years. It now has equipment of one sort or another working in many developing countries around the world. Much of this equipment is being used for land preparation and development in extremely harsh conditions where maintenance, if available, is often rudimentary. It is also being specified increasingly by large commercial operations that want a product that will give them high productivity with the minimum of downtime.

The ethos of this equipment is carried over into the light civil/construction product line, where the same requirement for strength, ease of operation and simplicity is paramount, especially where the equipment is likely to be working in remote areas with the minimum of backup support.

The light civil equipment manufactured by Simba falls into the following categories:

○ towed light and heavy-duty graders
○ lime stabilization equipment
○ tractor-drawn dead-weight road rollers
○ towed box scrapers.

If we examine this equipment in detail we see a common thread of design running through them, as follows:

○ All of the frames and chassis are manufactured from high quality thick walled rolled hollow section (RHS) tubing, or heavy-duty angle steel for strength and resistance to bending, but also for ease of repair in the event of a failure.
○ As much component commonality as possible is engineered into the design to simplify parts requirements and reduce the need locally for large stocks of spare parts.
○ Hydraulics are used only where absolutely necessary for the efficient operation of the equipment, or in cases where omitting it would place an unnecessary physical burden on the operator.
○ The amount of consumables or fast-moving parts are kept to a minimum.

○ The equipment is all non-powered, i.e. it does not have its own dedicated power supply, so it can be pulled with any suitable power source available locally, for example a farm tractor.

The beauty of a road maintenance system based around this equipment is simplicity coupled with productivity and the benefits of using a remote power source, which includes:

○ It is cheaper and does not tie up capital when not in use for a particular application.
○ The prime mover's cost can be spread over many operations, including general haulage, personnel transport and so on.
○ The prime mover can be replaced as and when required without the need to replace other equipment.

Towed grader

Perhaps the single most important item of intermediate equipment is the towed grader, which is one unit that can work in isolation. Towed graders have been developed to address the increasing need for a simple and inexpensive method of maintaining rural access roads in conjunction with local labour, rather than at the expense of local labour.

Large self-propelled motor graders are the perfect tool for creating a new road, but are generally considered too expensive and sophisticated for the occasional maintenance of that road. The towed grader was developed to take over from the motorized grader once it has finished the task of constructing a new road, and its on-going expense can no longer be justified.

In an increasing number of African states, it is recognized that to maintain roads using a small labour team in conjunction with a towed grader is cost efficient and effective. Typically this team would consist of:

○ 1 towed grader
○ 1 or 2 tractors of about 75–90 horsepower
○ 1 trailer, low enough to be hand filled
○ 1 towed road roller (optional)
○ 1 caravan for the team to sleep in.

This team can then move as an independent, self-sufficient group, which in total costs a fraction of one motor grader, and has the additional benefit of providing work for local labour and contractors.

Experience has shown that in 99 per cent of road maintenance cases, a heavy-duty grader model is required, for the following reasons.

○ The combination of in-built weight and the ability to accept additional ballast if required gives improved performance in hard underfoot conditions, and retains the stability associated with self-propelled graders, that have built-in ballast in the form of an engine and transmission.

○ The optional addition of a rear-mounted scarifier is important and improves versatility.

○ The ability to move higher blade loads improves productivity.

Of the three points raised above, sufficient weight is probably the most important factor. With additional in-frame and external ballast, the operating weight can be increased from a shipping weight of about 2750kg, to an operating weight of about 5750kg. This is sufficient to allow scarifier and mouldboard penetration in all but the hardest conditions. (Pre-ripping may still be necessary.)

Internal ballasting is achieved by constructing the main chassis from 200 × 200 × 10mm RHS that is flanged to allow ease of shipment, but also permits the insertion of any heavy material during assembly on site, or at the factory. An additional tonne of 'suitcase' style ballast weights can be mounted on the rear axle assembly if required, and finally the tyres can be foam filled, which gives the benefit of ballast and complete puncture-proofing.

The grader mouldboard is of either three or four metres in width (depending upon the final specification chosen) and can be rotated in line with the direction of travel for transport purposes. It is hydraulically operated via a simple spool valve mounted at the operator's station which is situated above the mouldboard, giving excellent visibility to the work area, and ease of operation.

Provision is made for fitting an optional rear-mounted ripper/scarifier which comes complete with five tines and replaceable points, and is operated via a single hydraulic cylinder controlled by a single lever from the operator's station.

Towed graders of this specification can be expected to renovate between one and two kilometres of road a day, depending upon prevailing conditions.

Disc harrows

To further improve the performance of a towed grader in very severe conditions the use of disc harrows should be considered as a means of 'softening up' the road surface prior to grading. The disc harrow can also be used for the more normal task of mixing a stabilizing material such as lime.

Disc harrows for this application require the following:

○ A minimum of 150kg/blade: sufficient weight to achieve penetration in hard conditions.

○ A robust frame with the ability to flex when working in difficult terrain: in this instance angle steel is better than box section, which is designed to withstand flexing.

○ Extremely robust and easily maintained bearings to support the disc axles.

These should be of taper roller design and grease-flushable with leather (not synthetic) seals. If greased on a daily basis they will allow any grit to be flush out from around the seal, keep the leather moist and provide long and trouble-free life.

○ A disc-to-disc spacing wide enough to allow material to flow through the harrow without undue blockage occurring. This would probably be no less than 305mm with a disc of 710mm diameter.

The Simba 'Hybrid' disc combines all of these elements but also has wider disc spacing on the rear gang of the implement compared to the front gang, together with a smaller disc diameter on the front gang compared to the rear gang. This achieves the objective of allowing less restricted flow of material through the harrow. It also achieves a better performance from the rear gang of discs which, being of larger diameter, are working in unmoved material and to a greater depth than the front discs, giving a progressively deeper cut, which is more efficient than a conventional disc in this application.

Dead-weight roller

The towed dead-weight roller should be as simple as possible, with a solid box frame and large bearings for the roller. These need not be sophisticated bearings as they are for a slow-moving implement, but preferably should be greasable on a regular (say daily) basis which ensures that maintenance is carried out.

For ease of movement between sites, a simple wheeled transport system can be incorporated which, with the aid of one hydraulic ram, will tilt the roller backwards onto a pair of wheels, transferring the roller weight on to the wheels and away from the towing vehicle. This reduces the need for counterweighting on the towing vehicle and allows a smaller size vehicle to be used for transporting if necessary.

If the roller is to be moved long distances between sites and is water or liquid ballasted, ideally this should be emptied out before making the journey, to prolong bearing life on the roller and to reduce overall stress on the towing vehicle. Rubber tyres are preferable to steel wheels for transport as they have a degree of cushioning and can be foam-filled to prevent punctures, further reducing the chance of downtime.

Other intermediate equipment

Additional equipment that may be applicable in certain countries and conditions would be towed bottomless box scrapers, which follow the same ethos as the equipment already discussed, and have the following characteristics.

○ They can provide simple grade maintenance or irrigation/runoff control.

○ They share the same principles of a separate prime mover and are virtually maintenance free.
○ They can be as simple or as complex as the task requires. The addition of laser equipment to the basic machine can, if required, provide levels of grade acuracy that cannot be achieved manually.

Finally, Simba 'Universal Toolbars' offer the contractor a simple and expandable system of tools to be used with the same basic prime mover, which can include various ripper tines, scarifier tines, mouldboards for drainage ditches, and so on. The basic 'ladder style' double beam toolbar is probably one of the most cost-effective implements as it can be adapted to so many tasks with a little imagination and the use of a welder!

CHAPTER 5

Intermediate equipment

L. Wedd

Travelling around the rural roads of East Africa, the observant traveller will be amazed at the number of road maintenance machines that lie by the roadside seemingly abandoned. The cause of this can be attributed to a number of factors. The most obvious one is the lack of money or spares – quite often the former leading to the latter. This is not the only reason; there are other, less obvious reasons, which could include the lack of knowledge on the part of the mechanic or operator. All of which must point to the need for simplicity, low-cost spares, and the ability to be able to fabricate as many parts as possible in the local field workshop. Most of the machines abandoned on the side of the road belong to government or parastatal organizations, seldom private enterprises.

Due to a change in the policy of firewood handling, The African Highlands Produce Company Limited (AHP) needed additional road-making equipment. The choice was between an expensive motor grader or a smaller tractor-drawn unit.

AHP started planting tea in the Kericho district in the early 1930s, and has continued to develop to the present. At present there are 5600 hectares of tea, 1700 hectares of eucalyptus (gum), 400 hectares of softwood and 40 hectares of flowers. The balance of 6000 hectares is taken up by labour villages, factory sites, riverine forest, roads, firewood stacking areas, a compost site, airstrips, houses and gardens. In 1995 the area under tea will produce in the region of 24 million kilograms of black tea and one million kilograms of instant tea, most of which is exported either directly or through the tea auctions in Mombasa. To dry this tea, eucalyptus is burnt in the 18 converted locomotive boilers. The steam from the boilers heats the air going into the fluid bed dryers; 1.6 kilograms of firewood is needed to dry one kilogram of tea. The softwood is cut into timber to build houses for the 16 000 labour force. Building blocks, roofing tiles, doors and windows are among the items produced to help make the company be as self-sufficient as possible. 40 per cent of the electrical power demand is generated by hydroelectric generators, the balance coming from the national grid. The older generators were installed in the early 1940s, while a more recent machine was installed in 1988. Insufficient water in the dry periods has prevented the installation of further hydroelectric power plants, but consideration is now being given to the installation of steam turbines. To provide standby power, a number of diesel generators have been purchased. Self-sufficiency is the aim, and in 1993 AHP won the Tate and Lyle award for conservation and the use of renewable energy.

Until 1993 all firewood had been transported to the factories from the field by farm tractors and trailers. The trees were felled on an eight year cycle, cut by power saw into one metre lengths, and then split by hand axe. These small billets were loaded on to the trailers by hand and transported to the factories. The damage to tyres and tractors made this a very expensive transportation method. In an attempt to improve efficiency, and reduce cost, a decision was taken to transport the logs in six-metre lengths on lorries, rather than by tractor-drawn trailers. The felled trees were to be winched to the road edge by double drum mounted winches or skylining. Both loading and unloading would be done by logging gabs. The cutting and splitting would now be done under better supervision in the factory compounds. This new operation would mean that roads suitable for lorries rather than tractors would have to be constructed in the eucalyptus (fuel) areas.

The AHP property is situated at an elevation of between 5500 and 7200 feet, on the west of the Rift Valley. The land is L shaped, with four river valleys splitting it into five main tea-producing areas. Gradients are very steep in some areas and it is on these slopes that the majority of gum is planted. A private tar road runs through the middle of property, while all other roads are gravel and are normally referred to as 'dirt' roads. Each year these roads carry the transport for well over 100 000 tons of green tea leaf, 25 000 tons of made tea, 38 000 tons of firewood 2500 tons of compost, 2000 tons fertilizer, and over 41 million cut flowers, plus management and private transport. In addition, the annual rainfall is in excess of 2000mm – the maintenance of roads is therefore crucial to the smooth running of the company's operation.

The total road system comprises 36 kilometres of surfaced (tar) roads, 130 kilometres of made-up dirt roads and 80 kilometres of grass roads. The grass roads receive very little maintenance other than the quarterly mowing. The tar roads need constant patching as they were built to take 5-ton trucks, but are now accommodating 40-ton articulated container transporters. It is the dirt roads that need most attention. This paper, while referring to roads in general, deals more specifically with the need to improve the gum roads.

Until the switch in firewood-handling policy, road maintenance was carried out with several tractor-drawn scrapers, an ageing Caterpillar 121 grader and various rollers. In 1994 AHP purchased a Simba tractor-drawn grader. For a company that was generally progressive and always looking to become more economical this change in direction may have appeared out of the ordinary. But a close look at the alternatives, bearing in mind that tea prices were not at all healthy, reveals that it is not surprising that the decision was made to go for something along the lines of the Simba grader.

The relative costs are shown in Table 5.1 below. While these act as a comparison, they are by no means comprehensive.

From the figures shown in Table 5.1 it can be seen that it is possible to put together a tractor and grader combination for about KSh 3,600,000. However, to buy a motor grader would cost in the region of 12 to 15 million shillings. For a small operation, or for use in rural areas, the advantage of being able to change the prime mover 'at the drop of a hat' must never be overlooked. AHP had several 80hp 4wd tractors left over from the original firewood collection system. The choice to go for the towed grader option was therefore not a difficult one.

It must be stated that the towed grader is not capable of directly replacing the motor grader, but in conditions where there is likely to be a problem with spares, maintenance, cost, or servicing it is often a better option, and it may be more productive in the long run, particularly as the machines get older, due in the main to the reduced down-time.

The move in AHP to go over to transporting by lorry meant that roads that formally carried tractors would now have to take lorries. The weight in the trailers was seldom over four tons, while the lorries were going to carry over 10 tons and in some cases 12 tons. A Bell Hauler with a capacity of 16 tons was purchased in order to compare the long-term cost of this against that of Indian 'Tata' lorries. The gum plantations are felled on an eight-year cycle so the need to make up roads is a gradual one spaced over the eight years that it takes for the trees to mature. There will always be the need for maintenance after that, in addition to the tea roads that make up the majority of the road network.

The soil in Kericho is unusually deep, with some peculiar characteristics. If

Table 5.1: Comparative costs of graders and tractors

Motor graders	Towed graders	Farm tractors
Cat 120 G KSh 11,126,313	Simba light duty KSh 1,500,000	M.F. 390 KSh 1,190,000
Cat 140 G KSh 15,234,393	Simba heavy duty KSh 2,500,000	Ford 68 hp 4WD KSh 1,500,000
Komatsu KSh 12,000,000	Simba hydraulic KSh 2,700,000	Ford 80 hp 4WD KSh 1,800,000
		Same 70 hp 4WD KSh 1,200,000

[US$1 = KSh 58 Jan. 1996]

left undisturbed it will soak up an enormous amount of water, and dry out very quickly, but if it is puddled it will retain water for long periods, making it unsuitable for roads. On AHP there is no suitable gravel (murram) for road building so there has been developed a system of using both broken stone and a clay material that will bind the broken stone. This clay soon turns to dust if used on its own, but when wet it holds the stones together very well. The broken stone acts as a wearing surface to prevent the clay blowing away in the dry periods, and also improves traction in wet weather.

The broken stone comes from the valleys, where it is blasted from the hillside. Some of the boulders are transported from the quarry to a crusher where they are broken into smaller stones for building and use on the tarmac road. Stones for use on dirt roads are broken by hand into 2" pieces, mostly by women, the wives of pluckers, who are paid under contract. This method is cheaper than crushing by machine, and the slightly larger size is not lost in the clay. Tippers transport both types of stone to site.

Murram is also 'mined' from the hillsides, quite often in the same areas as the stone. The material is first loosened by bulldozer and then loaded on to trailers by a front-end loader. The method of making up the roads will depend to some extent on the area and the weather. Generally the tall gum trees prevent the sun from penetrating to the road surface, so the operation must be timed for suitable weather, which in Kericho is far from predictable.

A bulldozer will initially clear any trees from the alignment of the new, or in some cases existing, road but as trees are a valuable commodity the number removed is kept to an absolute minimum. The felled timber is then taken away as firewood. Remaining stumps are transferred to a suitable site where the soil is removed, before the roots are split and sent to the factories as fuel. With the area now clear of trees the road is shaped, and run-off drains constructed. Home-made culverts are installed where they are required. A heavy vibrating roller compacts the earth, and this is considered a very important process as it gives a hard foundation as well as preventing the stone from being pushed into the soil. On completion of the compaction, a 4" layer of murram is spread on the shaped road and rolled as soon as possible before any water can turn the murram into a soggy mess that will take weeks to dry out. Once the murram is spread and rolled the water runs off and it dries quite quickly. This permits the second layer of murram and stone to be applied, which again must be spread and rolled before it can be allowed to get wet. The ratio of stone to murram is 1:2 but on inclines it may be increased to 1:1.

The success of this method of road building depends to a very large extent on the ability to grade and roll before the murram can get wet. It is normal to have rain in Kericho on most afternoons, so the road construction operations must be performed in the morning.

Making new gum roads has now been going on for a year, and while there are times when a motor grader would have been better suited to the job, the towed grader has had its advantages. It appears to be much cheaper to operate, and certainly much cheaper to run. It can be used in tight corners where the motor grader would have trouble manoeuvring, and due to its construction the operator is able to work closer to obstructions such as culvert heads etc. The towing tractor can be used on other tasks if the grader is not required; on the other hand, if the tractor breaks down, it is easily replaced by another unit. The Cat grader is very old, while the towed unit is new, so it is impossible to compare costs directly, but there is no doubt that the towed grader has worked far more hours in the past year than the Cat, mainly due to the down-time of the older unit. If the towed grader breaks down almost all repairs can be done on site, where as the Cat would normally require the purchase of expensive spares.

Experience suggests that an anti-flip hitch has an advantage over conventional swinging tow-bars or an auto pick-up hitch. Weight transfer does not seem to be an advantage.

In short, the use of a towed grader has a big advantage over motor graders in areas where money, spares, or technical expertise are in short supply.

CHAPTER 6

Labour-based roadworks:
private sector development

E. Ashong

Introduction

The economy of many developing countries is on the decline. Attempts to reverse this trend have led to the initiation of economic recovery programmes with attendant austerity measures. The socio-economic effects of economic recovery programmes need to be cushioned to avoid short-term economic hardships and long-term social upheavals. Most developing countries have identified the ineffectiveness of the Civil Service due to the lack of adequate logistic support as one of the core causes of the problem and have started shedding part of the government direct-labour force to the private sector. This redeployment exercise cannot be effective without vibrant private sector programmes to give adequate absorption of the redundant government labour force in order to cushion the obvious effect of this exercise. One of these private sector programmes which has the potential of high labour absorption is the Ghana labour-based road construction and maintenance programme.

Ghana embarked on an economic recovery programme in 1983, including privatization of State Owned Enterprises (SOE) and other public sector operations. A new labour-based road rehabilitation and maintenance programme with private sector participation was established in 1986. This project has absorbed quite a substantial part of the hitherto idle labour force from the government sector which had migrated to the hinterland after being redeployed. For the private sector to perform such a role there is a need for planned systematic training and capacity development with a view to enhance and tap the latent business ability of this sector to suit the intended purpose.

The Ghana experience

The labour-based road programme in Ghana using small-scale contractors started in 1986. To date 93 contractors have been trained and 54 have been equipped with the appropriate set of light-duty equipment at an average cost of US$150 000. About 1300km of roads have been rehabilitated using an average of 2000 work days per km. With a minimum daily wage-rate of about US$1.25, about US$3.25m has been injected into the rural economy so far. The economic effect of this injection in terms of upliftment of the social status of the rural people has been particularly beneficial.

Small-scale contractor development

Small-scale contractor development should be planned to fit into an overall programme of development. This is necessary to ensure that the private sector performs its support role efficiently at every stage of the development programme. The use of the private sector in labour-based works puts an extra technical supervisory role on the government supervising agency, which should always have the adequate internal capacity to perform this function

The Ghana Development Programme

The development and application of labour-based technology for road rehabilitation and maintenance in Ghana started in 1986 as the Department of Feeder Roads (DFR) component of the World Bank funded Fourth Highway Project. UNDP provided funds for the necessary technical support by the ILO. The programme had the following objectives:

○ improved accessibility to rural areas by large-scale application of cost-saving approaches to feeder road construction, improvement and maintenance through the use of local resources
○ creation of a capacity within the Department of Feeder Roads and a number of private contracting firms to apply cost-saving methodologies efficiently to road improvement and maintenance
○ creation of additional employment opportunities by the introduction of a cost-effective labour-based approach to feeder road construction, improvement and maintenance.

From the above programme objectives, a systematic and planned programme development in tandem with private sector development and involvement was inevitable.

The project objectives were achieved in three phases:

1. Training of individual supervisors from small-scale contracting firms plus foremen and engineers from DFR.
2. Developing capabilities of contracting companies by giving them 5km each of practical trial sites to run on their own under DFR supervision.
3. Company development through on-site training by giving to each qualified contractor from the second phase 20km of road per annum to rehabilitate.

The Ghanaian road construction industry, before the introduction of the labour-based programme, was monopolized by orthodox capital-intensive methods. Thus, as with the introduction of any new product into a monopolized market, this new technology met a hostile environment. To break this barrier and penetrate such a market there was a need for attitudinal change as well as training, starting with meetings with various interest groups. These meetings were followed by a careful field introduction of the project.

A three-stage process was used in the introduction of the technology. DFR considered this project as a policy experiment and therefore created an effective feedback mechanism and was always alert to respond and adapt to changes at any stage of the project. The three stages could be classified as pilot, demonstration and replication.

Pilot stage

The use of labour-based technology in road rehabilitation and maintenance was started in Kenya by the ILO. The Ghana model was to use small-scale contractors. Thus, although the efficiency of the technology could not be doubted, the same could not to said for using the private sector. This phase was therefore used to test the feasibility and acceptability of the innovations to the Kenyan model. New organizational arrangements and management procedures were tested.

The pilot project was started in Sefwi-Wiawso in the Western region of Ghana in 1987 and was managed by a team headed by a project engineer and an ILO technical adviser who reported directly to the Director of DFR.

During this stage seven contractors were trained, equipped and taken through the three training phases defined earlier. The following were addressed:

○ security, in terms of finance
○ time for establishment, diffusion of information and acceptance by participants
○ an understanding of and respect for the diversity of cultural values and norms found within communities, their willingness to change, and the degree of control that local people have over the factors that create, maintain, and alter those values
○ formal and informal authority relationships within communities taking part in the programme.

Project planning during this phase was flexible and responsive. Careful attention was paid to site selection, labour recruitment and the avoidance of conflict with local officials, political leaders and vested interest groups.

Demonstration

The demonstration stage of the labour-based programme started in 1990 by the expansion into two more regions, namely Ashant and Rrong-Ahafo. The purpose was to test how the organizational structures developed during the pilot phase would fare in different environments and away from the strict monitoring of the project team.

Six contractors were trained and equipped for each of the two regions. During this stage some of the advantages and autonomy of the pilot phase were withdrawn. This was to determine how the project would fare under stringent civil service rules. This phase was therefore necessary to build administrative capacity on small incremental, rather than large-scale and complex activities which have a higher probability of failing. This phase helped to determine the additional resources and manpower needed for full-scale expansion of the programme.

Replication and dissemination stage
This phase is the nation-wide expansion of the tested methods and techniques. The major aim of this phase is to expand administrative and productive capacity.

At this stage, the administration of the project was transferred to the normal DFR regional set-up. Each region had a project engineer for labour-based projects. In determining the rate of replication, the following factors were considered:

○ degree of DFR participation
○ quality of project staff
○ degree of financial support
○ strength of leadership and human resources in DFR.

The project is managed at head office level by a national co-ordinator under the Deputy Director (Development).

Contractor selection and training

Selection of contractors
The selection of labour-based contractors is a carefully planned exercise. Although the idea is to bring in small-scale contractors for training, it is necessary for them to meet certain conditions in the selection exercise to ensure success on the training programme. Prospective labour-based contractors are given a questionnaire with carefully designed questions for them to answer. Their responses are then weighted and used to assess the suitability of a contractor for the labour-based programme. Data gathered is put in block areas, such as financial status, work experience, vehicle and plant holdings and so on. This results in an evaluated short-list of contractors who enter a ballot for a place on the course.

Training contractors
Selected contracting firms undergo a period of training with the department.

Training contractors in the use of labour-based technology is carried out in three phases:

1. Initial training
2. Trial contract training
3. Standard contract training.

The most important phases are the initial and trial contract period of training. Actual knowledge and skills of the labour-based technology are imparted at the initial stage. This is then put on trial when areas of insufficiency in knowledge and skills can be corrected. The main focus has been on the initial training phase, which has been quite dynamic. It has gone through various forms, each time improving on a previous form.

The developmental stages of labour-based training

The content and duration of the training programme has gone through three major stages. These developmental stages were aimed at improving the course content in order to address certain particular problems that surfaced in the implementation of project. The location of the training school was moved from Sefwi-Wiawso in the North-western part of the country – a whole day's travelling time from Accra – to Koforidua in the Eastern region with a travelling time of just one-and-a-half hours from Accra. The major details of the training courses are included in Table 6.1.

The major changes which occured during the development of the courses were:

○ shorter duration
○ improved selection through tests and interviews
○ management training removed completely
○ introduction of new subject areas
   e.g. - soil technology/quantity control
        - survey (improved)
        - environmental issues.

Management courses

With assistance from the ILO, the department has designed two different types of management training programmes for managing directors and other senior managers. These courses have been specifically designed to address the needs of contractors. The first course is the Introductory Course aimed at newly-trained contractors. The second, Advanced Course, is meant for experienced contractors (firms that have been in business for not less than three years). The two courses each have a two-week duration covering the same subjects but with different content. Subjects covered are mostly in management and technical topics.

52

Table 6.1: Training course development 1987 to the present

Training location	Training dates	Course duration	No of participants	Basic text	Breakdown of course
Sefwi-Wiawso	(1987-1989)	23 weeks	24 (6 companies)	ILO manuals and GHA basic maths manuals	Six weeks classroom 2 weeks basic maths training 2 weeks technical training 2 weeks specialized training Sixteen weeks model road field training One week management training Human relations for MDs and managers plus back-up mechanical training
Koforidua	(1989-1993)	20 weeks	32	ILO manuals and GHA basic maths manuals	Five weeks classroom 1 weeks basic maths training 2 weeks technical training 2 weeks specialized training Fourteen weeks model road field training One week management training Human relations for MDs and managers
Koforidua	(1993-Present)	18 weeks	32	ILO manuals	Five weeks classroom No basic maths training Fourteen weeks model road field training One week maintenance training

Training achievements
Numbers of trained personnel:

○ contractors' staff 380
○ DFR engineers 64
○ DFR foremen 78
○ contracting firms 93
○ equipped firms 54

Development of literature
Although the ILO manuals remain the basic text material, attempts have been made to write a Ghana-specific manual for teaching purposes. However, there is a manual in modular form for the maintenance course. There are other handbooks for field supervisors which serve as quick reminders in times of need, and are also useful for guest lecturers. Handbooks also serve as a simplified 'training of trainers guide'.

Evaluation of training
Not much evaluation of the training programmes have been done formally, but occasional interactions with engineers and contractors have brought to the attention of the department areas of the technology that need modification. This has contributed on a larger scale to the changes that have taken place in the structure of the labour based courses run by the department. It has also shown the need to start running refresher courses for past trainees to bring them up to date with the latest developments in the technology.

The way ahead

The labour-based programme in Ghana has been in existence for about eight years. The number of contractors trained has increased from seven to 93 over this period. The consequences of such a fast expansion are becoming evident. Experience gained over the years has shown that there are some pitfalls which need to be addressed and avoided in any labour-based programme involving the private sector. The most important of these are as follows:

○ Politically-propelled over-expansion:
  This becomes inevitable when the programme has been accepted as a panacea for the solution of labour problems in the country. Care and diligence should, however, be taken into consideration in order not to sacrifice quality and not to allow the programme to become just an employment generating exercise.
○ Enough supervisory capacity of the executing agency:
  As the number of trained contractors increases, a corresponding number of supervisory staff of the executing agency should be trained. In the worst case there should be at least one supervisor to two contractors.

○ Follow-up training:
Enough prompt feed-back mechanisms should be put in place to enable the training division to respond to the needs of already trained foremen and supervisors. This will lead to the institution of corrective measures at the very early stages.
○ Geographical expansion:
This should be gradual, and should be matched to the available man-power and logistics ability.

Conclusion

The novelty of the labour-based programme in Ghana, like a good new product, has been able to penetrate the hitherto monopolistic Ghanaian construction industry. Having made its mark, the programme has won the support of all, especially the government, because it is in line with its privatization programme and has the added benefits of rural employment-generation leading to a reversal of the rural–urban migration. For cost-effective and sustainable private sector development and utilization in labour-based road programmes, a high premium needs to be placed on training and supervision. When the in-house capacity for supervision is out-run as a result of a fast expansion or an embargo over employment, the services of private consultants should be employed.

CHAPTER 7

Local contractor operations and appropriate technology roadworks

M. Broadbent

Introduction

MART covers one of ODA's current priority research areas, and therefore it has a specific interest in the 'reduction in costs for the construction, rehabilitation and maintenance of road infrastructure, and vehicle operations' in developing countries.

Labour-based (LB) technologies have been proved to be effective and economic on projects in a wide variety of countries over the past 20 years, and demand for advice and assistance on their implementation continues to grow.

It is nevertheless recognized that a number of key problem areas remain to be addressed. One current area of concern is the expansion of a capacity and capability within the private sector to undertake LB work programmes. In this respect, there is a belief that LB work could be undertaken even more cost effectively if an element of private sector competition could be positively injected into future initiatives. There is no doubt that the involvement of the private sector has so far been limited, with the result that there has also been a failure to mobilize entrepreneurial skills and create enterprises which could themselves develop improved techniques and provide lasting employment opportunities.

This paper examines some experiences and lessons regarding the introduction of local contractor operations in a number of developing countries. It is believed that many of these experiences are equally relevant to both LB and conventional private sector work programmes, but the lessons are intended to focus primarily on appropriate technology roadworks. The author strongly believes there are many serious questions to be positively addressed before a sustainable private sector LB roadwork programme can be launched with any degree of confidence. For this reason, it is considered necessary to examine over time and on a wide scale the emerging role of the private sector's involvement in roadwork programmes before focusing on the specific problems facing the potential LB contractor.

A general overview

It would be difficult to deny that the role of the private sector in roadwork programmes is anything more than a business operation. It is within this context that it should be recognized that any typical business operation would set out with an objective of achieving an optimum performance in its efficiency. A successful business is certainly not a charitable organization. Indeed, any modern business organization must adopt good management practices if it is to be successful, and a good roadwork contractor would be no exception. The key players in this business are jointly both the purchaser and consumer (the client, generally the government, representing the general interests of the road user – the general public) as well as the producer (the contractor). The critical motivating influence would without doubt be the profit margins of the private sector contractor.

An ideal business operation would entail the purchaser/consumer getting precisely what was required (e.g. a road built to standard, to price and on time) and the producer/contractor making an adequate profit, and certainly a profit which could further motivate the contractor to pursue this line of business with an ultimate prospect of achieving even greater success. The two parties to this business operation therefore have clear objectives for the outcome of the transaction: the client gets what is required at the correct price and the supplier is at least content with the profit made on the business transaction. But what initial mechanisms must be in place to promote such a relationship, and once this is in place, how can it be further strengthened and even made sustainable? Furthermore, what are the ultimate objectives for this line of business, and what can be learnt from successful traditional private sector operations which might be equally applicable to LB work programmes in the future?

There is little doubt that both road sector clients and their respective private sector counterparts operating in most developed Western economies have in the past enjoyed a productive and a relatively relaxed relationship. Achievements and outputs up to the present time have certainly been impressive, and most clients would probably feel that they have secured their products at a competitive price. Many contractors have made good profits, and furthermore, profits on a scale adequate both to promote and attract competition. These provisions have been met by the mechanisms of the market, supported by both technological developments and business management skills.

Within this market framework, the client has been able to specify precise requirements through a joint planning/ design process, the outcome of which is some form of tender document containing descriptions of the work, detailed drawings, specifications, bills of quantities together with intended contractual provisions covering conditions of contract, forms of agreement etc. This tender process is a key element in the ultimate production objective, as it provides both the client an opportunity for the client to review whether there are adequate resources to proceed with the task and, at the same time, an opportunity for prospective contractors to assess whether they have both the capacity and the capability to satisfy the objectives of the commission. Furthermore, both parties have a critical opportunity to assess the financial cost of making a commitment. The prospective client is able to review whether the price is competitive and attractive; the prospective contractor whether the commission is likely to provide an adequate profit element within the bid offer to retain the business in a healthy financial position.

This framework of client/contractor relationships has progressed over time to build an impressive industry which even today continues to be subject to the pressures of change in response to the needs of the market. Indeed, the process in the industrialized Western economies has progressed to cater for the needs of both large and small capital project works; large and small road maintenance commissions; competition in the planning/ design process: and most recently, even competition in the field of large consolidated design/construct packages. In parallel with these initiatives, which have all set out to provide even more competition, and therefore, in theory, a better financial deal for the client, additional developments have taken place which have concentrated on the development of more appropriate tender/contractual arrangements. Improved contractual arrangements appear to have one overriding objective, namely an improved control of works for the lowest financial outlay to the mutual benefit of all parties, and this has set out to cater both for large as well as small-scale operations. In line with such initiatives, the 'Multilateral Flagship – i.e. the FIDIC Model Conditions of Contract' continues to be fine tuned, and supplementary documents have been developed for specific use on small-scale works. Additional initiatives have also been taken to strengthen the working relationships between the contractual parties, with a greater emphasis on the team approach to resolving problems under contractual obligations.

But what is the relevance of these observations to the expansion of the private sector capacity on LB roadwork programmes? It could certainly be argued that the massive changes in the conventional approach to undertaking work programmes by the private sector have been taking place in the West while many of the recognised LB programmes in Africa and the Far East have seen relatively little change since early initiatives were taken some 20 years ago. Although new initiatives have been, and continue to be, taken on many LB roadwork programmes, it is clear that no major breakthroughs have taken place which would enable LB work programmes to be implemented by the private sector both on a sustainable basis as well as under the sole financing of domestic local funding! The author is of the opinion that these two issues are of critical importance.

Furthermore, whereas it is clear that multilateral agencies such as the World Bank have taken initiatives to develop the domestic contracting industry in a number of developing countries, much of this has focused on the conventional approach to work programmes, and only limited provisions have been made for LB roadwork programmes. Moreover, it is equally clear that only limited progress has been achieved even on the conventional work programmes, and therefore a radical new approach is probably required if there is to be any prospect of launching a successful initiative of expanding the private sector capacity on LB work programmes.

The identification of the necessary ingredients for the new approach is probably the most critical issue facing future initiatives. Clearly, much can be learned from experiences to date both under traditional/ conventional as well as LB work programmes undertaken by the private sector, but it also appears equally essential to take careful note of the total technology know-how that has been built up on LB work programmes over the last 20 years when considering the potential future opportunities.

The appropriate technology of labour-based roadworks

Most LB roadwork programmes were launched with clear objectives. Many set out with the objectives of improving the standards of rural infrastructure and providing employment opportunities for the rural poor and the underemployed. In the first instance, therefore, most of the emphasis was placed on the construction and improvement of rural unpaved roads carrying relatively low traffic volumes, but over time the emphasis has shifted to the essential needs of maintenance and related essential spot improvements. Clearly, to satisfy the objectives a high percentage of work has been undertaken by organized labour gangs, but certain activities have been supported by intermediate forms of equipment where this has proved to be desirable. This implementation strategy continues to be adapted and improved with the objective of catering even for the needs of entire road networks.

A high percentage of LB construction and spot improvement work programmes have to date been financed under force account budget provisions, and have adopted 'recipe' methods in work implementation practices. Clearly, there are exceptions. The recipe method appears to be fundamentally correct in many respects, since relatively little effort is required in making preparations for work implementation. This statement could be grossly misinterpreted, but it is significant. The method approach certainly avoids the costs of topographical site surveys and the preparation of alignment designs and related drawings. Such provisions are both costly and demand skills which may not be readily available, and moreover, is there a need to quantify precisely the alignment criteria for an unpaved rural road. Furthermore, the available funding is channelled into productive employment from the onset, and it could be argued this is a highly desirable feature of the method approach.

In contrast, the method approach has many drawbacks for a traditional client/contractor relationship in which an element of competition as well as profit was being sought. The client would certainly not be able to quantify the precise requirements without a design, and the contractor would be unable to provide a price estimate – and therefore a competitive bid – developed from a quantified work programme. Furthermore, the client would lose some financial flexibility that is automatically afforded in force account work, since once a contract is in place, the full financial provisions are committed. Clearly, there are many questions that require detailed attention.

Road construction/rehabilitation/improvement provisions are individually one-off events, and are therefore clearly specific in nature. In contrast, maintenance activities are a continuous operation and are the consequence of a necessary response to the inevitable deterioration of unpaved roads – in particular, low-cost unpaved rural roads. The demands of rural road maintenance are particularly suited to LB work programmes, but it must be recognized that there is a difficulty in quantifying the precise nature of work requirements as this is constantly changing on a day-to-day basis. None the less, many LB work programmes have now developed an approach for effective force account maintenance on unpaved rural roads, but it remains debatable how feasible it is to make this approach really efficient. Maintenance work carries little glamour, and is a thankless task with little reward. The work can be disperse, difficult to manage, organize, administer, supervise, control and is certainly complex to quantify. Consequently, a client may feel there is good reason why maintenance work could beneficially be assigned to the private sector, provided this could be made attractive, and an element of competition stimulated. Clearly, a major attraction of maintenance work would be that it is essential and therefore this represents a potential workload with no end; it is continuous; it does not require completed equipment for many activities on unpaved rural roads, etc.

However, many traditional contractors find typical small-scale road maintenance operations unattractive, for many of the reasons already mentioned. This is understandable. The work can be awkward to organize and plan systematically, and for this reason, contractors generally find it difficult to motivate their personnel. Furthermore, attractive profits are not readily generated from many of the typical operations unless work is undertaken in a deliberately substandard manner. The author has noticed that many simple yet cost-effective maintenance operations are purposely not undertaken as efficiently as is feasible, since some contractors would prefer to see a road deteriorate at a very rapid rate. This approach accelerates the timing of the next major intervention, such as periodic regravelling or even rehabilitative measures, and since such operations are high cost, they are much more attractive to the contractor. Such provisions necessitate both strict standards and performance criteria, together with strict supervisory controls. But even these provisions can clearly be very costly.

Many of the arguments presented which set out to justify an LB approach to spot improvement and maintenance works can be difficult to quantify objectively. But LB works represent both a pragmatic and sustainable approach, certainly in the rural areas where traditional operations can be virtually non-productive, or of a low quality. It is therefore clear there is a good case to be argued for making a major thrust to improve the current status of LB work programmes undertaken by the private sector. But where should initiatives be taken in the developing countries, bearing in mind the need to ensure that future programmes are sustainable, and the need to ensure that not too much reliance is placed on long term donor funding for essential day-to-day maintenance operations. The key to these questions can probably be found by examining some experiences and findings on roadwork programmes in a number of developing countries. The following case studies set out to illustrate the range of constraints as well as opportunities. Since some of the issues may be sensitive to the host governments of some developing countries, as well as of prejudice to future efforts, the specific locations of work programmes have deliberately not been specified.

Some experiences and lessons on roadworks programmes

The experiences and lessons presented in some of these case studies are not entirely specific to LB work programmes, but they are considered to be relevant, and are therefore included for guidance purposes.

Case Study 1: An island in the Caribbean

This case study concerns a major road improvement and maintenance pro-gramme supported by the World Bank. A major component of the works programme concerned the strengthening of paved road networks under con-tract (funded by the Bank), but with initial preparatory work to existing pavements being undertaken in advance of the contract works by force account (funded by the host government). The force account operations were delayed routine maintenance operations, and concerned a high degree of local patching and reconstruction of local pavement failures. In the event that the force account operations were either delayed or not implemented, provisions were made in the contract for such works to be undertaken by the contractor. Clearly, such provisions were essential, as potential delays to the major contract works, for whatever reason, could have proved costly in terms of contractual produc-tion losses.

Although not officially recognised to be an LB work programme, the preparatory force account work programmes had many similarities to the international practices of official LB technology. The force account work programmes suffered from delays in funding; breakdowns in small items of equipment (i.e. hand vibrating roller); inadequate progress to keep ahead of the contractors' programme; and a lack in the motivating mechanisms to correct these shortcomings. All these shortcomings highlight some of the critical difficulties in force account work practices, which ultimately can only be reflected in the potential cost savings and performance criteria expected from the private sector.

The contractors were therefore instructed, from time to time, to undertake the preparatory pavement work activities in accordance with the provisions of the contract, which was based on FIDIC. This initiative ensured that the major work programme was not subject to major disruption, but it must be emphasized that the contractor disliked intensely the nature of the preparatory work, and did virtually everything to avoid it. The rates for the preparatory work were certainly more than adequate, but were not attractive when compared to the profit margins generated by the major work. Consequently, this situation necessitated a strong supervisory role, with firm management and technical skills to ensure the work was up to standard.

An additional interesting observation concerns the adoption of the FIDIC Conditions of Contract for the works. These had not be used before, and a training programme was provided in connection with their application and use both for the local contractors and the supervisors. It was clear that the domestic market had no interest whatsoever in FIDIC. The senior management of the contractor certainly made no serious effort to understand FIDIC, but depended on the advice of Caribbean lawyers as to whether the provisions could create any problems. The works were eventually completed, but the local contractors never understood their obligations. Moreover, an outcome of the initial tranche of these contract works undertaken by local contractors was the difficulty in generating a positive response of interest in undertaking future contract works under FIDIC, even though this provision was a requirement stipulated by the loan agency, the World Bank. Clearly, an initial objective of the work was to expand the private capacity and capability of the domestic contracting industry; in the event, the initiatives probably went far in *reducing* the capacity and capability!

Case Study 2: A country in the Far East with a fast growth economy

A great deal of major development as well as massive work undertakings in this country have been undertaken by the private sector within a competitive environment, with funding provided from both domestic sources as well as multilateral/ bilateral sources. In recent years, initiatives were also taken to launch a national LB roadwork programme with the assistance of UNDP in collaboration with the ILO.

Some 10 years ago, the Ministry of Finance instructed all government departments to adopt a form of tender/conditions of contract which had been developed specifically for the needs of the country, reflecting the culture and work practices of the East. These conditions were to be applied to all major works, whether they were to be funded under local programmes or from an external source. It was the express wish of this government that the FIDIC

Conditions of Contract should not be used, as there was an opinion that FIDIC, based on past experience, provided a favourable advantage to the contractor. Furthermore, the government, in the capacity of a financial borrower, also considered that the lender and borrower should be equally bound to the financial risks of project works implementation. For such circumstances, the FIDIC Conditions of Contract are totally inappropriate. Yet it is clear that many major successful undertakings with technical complexities have been completed throughout the country, to a standard at least equivalent to that which would be attained in the West, and the client and contracting industry are equally content with the outcome.

The LB rural road programme was launched in this rapid developing economy. The objectives of the works programme were common to most LB projects, and were undertaken by force account. The works set out to address both the needs of construction and maintenance virtually from the outset. Financial resources for all works programmes were provided in their entirety by government. Furthermore, the LB programme was requested to expand the scale of its operations to absorb additional levels of domestic funding to satisfy the favourable developments of the programme and its desirable objectives. But the LB programme resisted the temptation to expand its operations faster than its capacity to build its capability, and consequently the scale of operations was purposely constrained. In response to this development, the LB programme was requested to investigate the potential for expanding its scale of operations through the use of the private sector.

In parallel with these developments, other rural road programmes – adopting both traditional and conventional work practices – were making preparations for expanding the scale of their operations in response to the availability of additional funding. One programme adopted force account procedures using an ageing fleet of plant for which a policy decision had been taken not to provide replacements from imported sources. This programme elected to develop locally-manufactured intermediate forms of equipment, adopting a towed grader powered by a locally attached engine unit. In contrast, the other major rural road programme elected to make full and detailed preparations for expanding its commitments using the extensive traditional capacity of the private sector. An extensive programme for budgeting, planning, surveying, design and tender documentation preparations was launched and successfully completed, but not one single contract was ever awarded. This situation arose from the fact that there was a surplus of work opportunities for private sector contractors within the market, and this work was far more attractive than the potential financial rewards for any remote rural road programme.

Needless to say, the LB rural road programme elected not to explore the possibility of expanding its commitments over the short term, recognizing that the issues were complex even for the traditional and conventional approaches to the desired work level. It was recognized that a great deal of careful judgement would be required to ensure the private sector involvement in LB work programmes could be launched successfully, and thereafter made sustainable.

Case Study 3 : A country in East Africa

A number of East African countries have demonstrated over the years highly successful LB road programmes. However, a high percentage of the work has to date been undertaken by force account, even though interesting variations have recently been introduced. A general weakness in developments appears to be a general lack of a motivated domestic contracting industry, particularly medium to small-scale firms, and the lack of domestic financial resources. Perhaps there has also been too high a reliance on grant-funded external assistance, and furthermore, LB programmes driven by the conditions of the donor rather than for the best long-term interests of each recipient country.

Initiatives have to date been taken to involve the private sector in LB work programmes targeted at two levels, although efforts have been, and continue to be, taken to expand into other groupings. On the one hand, routine maintenance has been undertaken by individual contractors, who have been engaged under very simple one-page contracts. The productive performance of the current lengthman system continues to be the subject of debate, and clearly there is room for improvement. Furthermore, the current system necessitates a high degree of supervisory involvement, and it would be preferable to reduce the scale of this operation. On the other hand, LB preparatory rehabilitative and periodic regravelling works have also been undertaken by the private sector, but many of these initiatives are still very much in their infancy. In contrast to the simple one-page lengthman contract, these works have been undertaken in accordance with very comprehensive tender/contract documentation, based on FIDIC and work schedules prepared specific for LB programmes. These programmes have involved intense prequalification/ training components for potential LB contractors, and furthermore, a high degree of costly technical assistance provisions. Moreover, most works have been funded by donor assistance, and desirable continuity provisions have been lacking. Such provisions are essential prerequisites for a sustainable private sector involvement.

Recent initiatives have also been considered for undertaking LB work programmes using lease-hire arrangements for intermediate forms of equipment. Clearly, this may prove a desirable development, but it seems a sensible time to question whether a comprehensive FIDIC Conditions of Contract is really appropriate for this type of work; whether very detailed schedules and quantities of work requirements are needed for the tender exercise; and whether large-scale technical assistance provisions are essential or even desirable, particularly if there is to be a realistic wish to move to a sustainable situation in the shortest possible time. LB work programmes would certainly seem to be the appropriate answer to satisfy the day-to-day needs of road maintenance, with perhaps provisions for spot improvements. Clearly, such programmes must be sustainable; resources, even if not totally adequate, must be continuously available; and the institutional frameworks must be developed to ensure the tender/contract processes are simple if the capacity and capability of the private sector is to be successfully expanded. But where should the future initiatives focus to ensure the desirable provisions can be gradually expanded over time; the greatest impacts created with no major irreversible setbacks; and the objectives kept on course with allowances for refinements during the entire development process? For this, the author is clear that a major target should be set at the ultimate development of a very large number of small-scale contractors widely dispersed across the network of roads to be maintained. The LB works programmes would set out to cater for small improvement work packages such as a culvert, a small bridgework, a new drainage/embankment, some spot regravelling etc., and maintenance catering for the needs of 10-20km of routine maintenance. But how can this be best mobilized to satisfy the ultimate objectives? To answer this and other questions, it is probably necessary to pool further information from the experiences of further case studies.

Case Study 4: Labour-based work in some other countries

Many roadwork programmes in the Indian sub-continent have been undertaken in the past by many small-scale contractors with very few resources such as equipment, finance etc. Such works have normally been packaged into many small contracts. A critical feature of the tender/contract award process is that the work provisions are based on a schedule of priced quantities prepared by the client, based on published national rates, and the contractor is only required to assess one percentage variation to the total assessed cost for the tender submission. The contract is awarded to the most favourable percentage: a 'one figure' tender! Clearly, there are many drawbacks to this approach, but the process provides an element of competition; it is quick and uncomplicated; and it is very suitable for maintenance contracts on unpaved roads, particularly low traffic rural roads.

A successful LB programme involving the private sector has been undertaken in West Africa. This programme had the full support of both the host government and the international donor community. Provisions were made for potential contractors to obtain favourable commercial bank loans for launching initiatives to break into the work opportunities in the private sector. Loan provisions were particularly attractive for the purchase of capital equipment items. However, a close scrutiny of the contractual provisions would indicate these to be unduly complicated for typical small-scale LB work programmes. Furthermore, this approach appears to place too great a risk of a potential financial burden on an emerging private sector, particularly when there are no firm provisions in place to provide long-term commitments of work opportunities. It is necessary only to compare the current exposure of the contracting industries in the developed Western economies to appreciate the potential risks for an emerging private sector involved with this scale of operation.

Conclusions

This paper has examined in outline some experiences and lessons learnt on road programmes undertaken by both force account as well as the private sector. A focus has been made on the potential problems of expanding the capacity and capability of the private sector in the implementation of works adopting LB methods. The author is of the opinion that a completely new initiative is required which recognizes the specific constraints to potential local contractors operating within the environment of a developing country. The issues to be addressed are debatable, but some critical factors are presented here for ongoing assessment and review.

It is recommended that a suitable strategy for launching and expanding a sustainable LB roadwork programme for private sector involvement should focus on the following issues:

○ Identify a network of rural unpaved roads which it is envisaged will require both maintenance and spot improvement interventions for many years into the future.

○ Identify the scale of funding likely to be available over the long term for the type of works envisaged, and develop very simple tender/ contract documents for the works, including appropriate LB method specifications, priced bills of quantities for predicted works, covering the provisions of both maintenance and spot improvement.

○ Promote, market, educate and offer simple on-the-job training to local skilled labour in parallel, where possible, with current force account operations, and prepare for qualifying tenderers, tendering adopting a 'one figure' percentage approach for the award of contracts for small-scale operations (e.g. 10-20km maintenance and limited spot improvements) with a duration of between one and two years.

○ Set up local supervisory provisions with responsibility for regular reviews of progress; identifying defects and defining needs; setting standards; checking quality outputs; agreeing quantity of work outputs; agreeing on payment certificate; and initiating payment.

○ Monitor the performance of the road and recommend future timing for retendering.

○ Keep under constant evaluation the rate at which the capacity of the private sector can be expanded, together with the necessary changes to reflect the capability developments.

CHAPTER 8

Labour-based contractor
training project in Kenya

F. Karanja

Background and objectives to the project

The Labour-Based Contractor Training Project (LBCTP) in Kenya got under way in 1991 when the Ministry of Public Works and Housing (MOPWH) in conjunction with Swedish International Development Authority (SIDA) decided to train a number of contractors who would make use of the abundant labour in Kenya's rural areas for road improvement and maintenance works. The main objective was to establish guidelines for the selection, training and supervision of small, local contractors in labour-based gravelling operations through the implementation of about 96km of gravelling contracts for the minor roads programme (MRP) in some four districts in Central Province of Kenya and one district in Eastern Province of Kenya .

The minor roads programme is a large-scale labour-based road improvement and maintenance programme which normally addresses the low-volume rural roads in high agricultural potential districts in Kenya. This programme was started in 1987 and succeeded the rural access roads programme (RARP) which started in 1974. The minor roads programme is presently responsible for the maintenance of 8000 kilometres of rural access roads which were built under the RARP and about 3500 kilometres of minor roads (includes secondary (D), and minor (E) road classes and also some special-purpose roads such as wheat, sugar, tea and settlement roads) which have been improved since 1987. All these roads have been constructed or rehabilitated to gravel or earth standard using labour-based methods.

The majority of the improvement and maintenance work has been carried out by directly employed casual labour (force account) using labour-based techniques. In some special cases, a proportion of the gravelling of minor roads and regravelling of rural access roads has been carried out by contractors. This has been done for two main reasons:

○ The haul distance for the gravel from the quarry to a particular road is too long (more than 10km) for the standard minor roads programme tractor-trailer gravelling units.

○ The gravelling output required in a particular district and year is beyond the capacity of the minor roads programme gravelling units.

The gravelling contractors employed by the minor roads programme in the past have all used equipment-based techniques, particularly for quarry excavation and loading. However, based on the minor roads programme experience, the Ministry concluded that labour-based techniques could be competitive in most situations. Some of the reasons which made the Ministry consider promoting labour-based gravelling contracting were:

○ to generate more rural employment, which is consistent with the existing minor roads programme objectives
○ to promote the growth of small-scale local contractors who would be available to compete for future contract work under the minor roads programme and other programmes
○ to bring the skills and experience developed in labour-based techniques by the minor roads programme into the private sector
○ to counteract the existing shortage of appropriately equipped contractors for road gravelling, which was gradually leading to a lack of competition and high contract rates.

Methodology for project implementation

The issue of project administration was discussed between the Ministry and SIDA. Due to lack of adequate capacity in the Ministry to supervise such a project, and considering that it was relatively new ground, it was decided to use a consultant to provide the project support base, and also in the execution of the project. This was found to be a good idea because the consultant was going to be used to develop independent guidelines for the selection, training and supervision of the contractors, which would be discussed with SIDA and the Ministry.

Scope of work
The consultant was given the responsibility for the day-to-day administration of the contracts as well as the development and testing of guidelines for use in labour-based gravelling operations for the minor roads programme. The consultant was required, among other things, to do the following:

○ identify suitable contractors, or potential contractors
○ establish what training (method, duration and content), if any, is necessary for the contractors including the contractor's supervisory staff and for the minor roads programme supervisory staff

○ liaise with the minor roads programme training school at Kisii to organize the necessary training
○ develop appropriate contract documents for labour-based gravelling
○ develop guidelines for selection of contractors, bearing in mind the Ministry's preference for competitive bidding wherever possible
○ recommend appropriate contract-sizes and time periods
○ prepare individual contracts
○ evaluate tenders and recommend to SIDA/MOPWH contractors for appointment
○ supervise the contracts with the assistance of minor roads programme personnel
○ monitor contracts and provide advice and guidance to the contractors as necessary
○ develop an appropriate system by using or adapting the minor roads programme standard reporting forms
○ select suitable trial sites
○ negotiate and agree with selected contractors methods for reimbursement and compensation to gravel pit owners
○ execute all payments arising out of the training programme.

The training programme was planned to cover a 16-month period from January 1992 to April 1993, at which time the contractors and their supervisors were expected to have gone through both the theoretical and practical training, and some five contracts were to have been awarded through competitive tendering. KSh 20 million (Swedish Kronor 4.515 million) was set aside for the project.

Project implementation

Demonstration site
A demonstration road site of 7 km was selected in Muranga District in Central Province and one experienced contractor was given a test contract to try out various methods of carrying out labour-based gravelling works. This was done through the use of fixed rates. The experience gained from this exercise was considered important in determining viable working procedures. The demonstration road contract was carried out between November 1991 and March 1992.

Advertisement and selection of trainees
Meanwhile, while the demonstration contract was going on, an advertisement was placed in the local dailies for interested firms to apply for training as labour-based contractors. The only basic requirement for the applicants was the need to own at least two serviceable 7-ton flat bed or tipper trucks for

haulage of gravel. This requirement was necessary because transportation of gravel materials was expected to be the only mechanized operation in the labour-based gravelling works. The contractors were also required to appoint their own foremen, who would be interviewed and trained as supervisors for the contractors.

Of the 64 firms which responded to the advertisement 26 were short-listed for interviewing, and finally 12 were selected for the training. The interviews were conducted by a team consisting of the consultant, the MOPWH and the International Labour Organization (ILO). Interviews were also conducted for foremen trainees, and twelve were selected.

In order to short-list the contractor applicants, the following factors were taken into account, and points given on a pro rata basis:

Availability of haulage equipment
Proof of ownership was needed through the production of registration log books. Equipment was weighted based on age as follows:

0-1 year	10 points
1-2 years	9 points
up to	
9-10 years	0 points
(Maximum for equipment	20 points)

Educational attainment
Proof of educational level attained was required by the production of certificates. The following point-awarding criteria were used:

Secondary Education Div. III or Higher	5 points
Higher School Education (Form 6)	5 points
Professional training of any type	5 points
Civil Engineering Ordinary National Diploma	5 points
Civil Engineering HND or degree	10 points
(Maximum for educational attainment	20 points)

Residence
The applicant was allocated more points if his business residence was in the selected district. The points were awarded as follows:

Business residence in selected district	20 points
Business residence outside selected district	10 points
(Maximum for business residence	20 points)

Supervisory capacity
The foremen proposed by the firms for training were evaluated on the following criteria. The minimum age was put at 23 years, basic education was put at Secondary Education Div. III or above and the CVs provided were

70

supported by copies of certificates or diplomas:

Age 23-26 years	2 points
27-32 years	5 points
33-38 years	2 points
Over 38 years	0 points
Education Secondary Div. III	1 point
Trade Test III	1 point
Trade Test II	1 point
Trade Test I	5 points
Teacher training or equivalent	5 points
Ordinary Diploma	8 points
Experience in road works	
In each year	1 point
In maximum years	5 points
Former RARP/MRP Supervisors	5 points
(Maximum for supervisory capacity	20 points)

Experience in gravelling works
The applicant contractors were awarded more points if they proved that they had been involved in gravelling works before. The points were awarded as follows:

Every 5km of roads gravelled	1 point
(Maximum for experience	20 points)

After the short-listing, the applicant contractors and the foremen went through interviews and written tests and the selection for training was based on the following criteria:

Marks achieved in short-listing	40%
Performance of contractor in written test	30%
Performance of contractor in interview	15%
Performance of foreman in written test and interview	15%

The short-listing and selection of the contractors and foremen revealed that there was an ample number of potential gravelling contractors with adequate haulage capacity. However, a severe lack of capable supervisors was identified. Only a few contractors proposed sufficiently qualified candidates for the foremen training. For this reason, the contractors were ranked without considering the supervisory capacity among the criteria. The contractors were provided by the consultant with a foreman's job description to guide them in sending new proposals. Since not all contractors were able to provide the required supervisory staff, an advertisement was again placed in the local dailies for interested foremen to apply for the course. The trained foremen would later get an opportunity to be employed by the successful contractors.

Training

Contractors

The contractors went through a two-week theoretical training course at the labour-based, Kisii Training School (KTS) in May 1992. During this time one contractor dropped out. The course covered all technical and management aspects of labour-based gravelling methods. The course was followed by site visits to on-going gravelling works in Central Province of Kenya. Four seminars were also held to discuss in greater length the contracting and work procedures in the field. Between August and December 1992, the contractors were each given a 3km section where they were trained and closely guided on the works. They were paid fixed-rate contract terms. These contracts were of about KSh 500,000 each.

After completing the trial sections, the contractors were taken through some training in tendering in January 1993. They were then subjected to their first competitive tendering exercise. The consultant selected road projects which did not require substantial additional works beside light reshaping. During the competitive tendering some contractors won jobs, while others did not. When evaluating these tenders, the following assessment criteria were used:

Performance, Training Stage I (KTS)	10%
Performance, Training Stage II (on the Job)	30%
Pricing for 'Assignment' project	60%

Care was taken to discourage underquoting by setting a limiting price, which was a percentage below the engineer's estimate. Below this limiting price, the tender was considered too risky and the tenderers would be disqualified.

At the end of the evaluation exercise, six out of eleven tenders were selected and contracts were awarded. These contracts were of the magnitude of about KSh 1.5 million each. At the end of the trial contracts, an analysis of the trainee contractors showed that two particular contractors had done very poorly and these were therefore disqualified and were not awarded 'certificates of successful completion' of the training course. Nine contractors were therefore successful.

In May 1993, the nine qualified contractors were invited to tender for a second gravelling assignment and seven contracts were to be awarded. This time the tenders were evaluated on the following criteria:

Performance during training stage II (on the job training)   10%

Performance during assignment I project	10%
Pricing of assignment II project	80%

The training consultants then went through the 'negotiation stage' with the successful contractors to try to further reduce the contract sums. Negotiations were successful with six of the contractors but failed with one of them. Further negotiations were undertaken until an agreement was reached.

The contractors successfully completed the 'second assignment' gravelling jobs, after which they were considered mature and free to compete for future labour-based gravelling jobs in any district in the country.

Foremen
Of the foremen interviewed, 12 were selected for training. These went through 17 weeks of training at Kisii Training School, after which they were allocated to the various contractors. The training covered all the technical and management aspects of labour-based gravelling methods.

Two foremen dropped out during the training, leaving ten foremen to be allocated to eleven contractors. Two contractors were therefore forced to share a foreman. The ten foremen were able to complete their course successfully and were awarded certificates at the same time as the contractors in May 1993.

Ministry's engineers and inspectors
Various seminars were held for the Ministry's labour-based engineers and inspectors to enable them to manage efficiently the type of labour-based contracts that were developed during the contractor training project. The seminars were aimed at guiding the engineers and inspectors through the contract preparation, evaluation and implementation stages of actual contracts that they would be expected to award in the future.

At the end of these seminars, the engineers and their senior supervisory staff had gained the necessary capability to handle all labour-based gravelling and regravelling contracts. All the contracts which are in progress at present were prepared and tendered by the Ministry's engineers themselves.

The future
The nine contractors who successfully completed their training in labour-based contracting were registered with the Ministry as 'labour-based contractors in road construction'.

In the SIDA-funded districts, the Ministry set aside some gravelling/regravelling work for labour-based contracting between 1994 and 1997, for contractors registered in labour-based gravelling.

Meanwhile, the Ministry has reached an agreement with SIDA to train another group of contractors in Western Kenya within a two-and-a-half year period. Ten contractors are expected to be trained, including 12 foremen and

20 assistant foremen in order to have enough supervisory personnel whom the contractors can employ in their future work.

The Ministry wishes to increase the use of contractors in road maintenance in the future. In this regard, there will be a need to carry out some trial contracting in routine maintenance works. Not much work has been done in the country to determine how routine maintenance works can be contracted out. The following needs to be done in this area:

○ Expand the current routine maintenance 'lengthman' contracting (where each person is given about 1.5km to maintain) to petty-contracting where a single petty contractor could be in charge of several roads or kilometres of road and would employ some casual workers to carry out routine maintenance work.
○ Prepare simple contract documents for the petty contractors and also lay down clear administrative, measurement and payment procedures, and also obligations of the employer and the contractor.
○ Train people who are willing to work as petty contractors in all aspects of routine road maintenance. This would best be done through a consultancy and would require class and field training and also seminars to discuss issues and exchange ideas on how to improve efficiency.

The Ministry also expects contractor-training in both gravelling, regravelling and resealing works to gain speed as the country endeavours to increase private sector involvement in the maintenance of the road network. This is an area where the donor community can play an important role if the country is to be self-reliant in the highly competitive contracting industry.

Possible ways of enhancing labour-based construction in Kenya

At the present time Kenya is lucky to be endowed with a substantial number of supervisory and technical people of various levels of competence and training, who have in the past, in one way or another, been involved in the labour intensive RARP and MRP. There are engineers, inspectors (or technicians), overseers, headmen and others who have been supervising and checking technical standards and specifications in the field for the two programmes for the last twenty years.

The country is undergoing public sector reform, and several government employees are opting for early retirement from the public service. A number of these people are highly trained in road building and maintenance, with a large part of them working in labour-intensive programmes. It is therefore certain that in this group of people there lies a pool of potential contractors and/ or supervisors for contracts involving labour-based road improvement and maintenance. All that is required is to provide them with appropriate incentives and training or retraining in labour-based contracting. The following are some of the possible ways that can be used to encourage the growth of labour-based contracting.

Comprehensive review

A comprehensive review needs to be undertaken of the quantities and types of roadworks carried out in the roads department each year, their costs and financing, implementation methods (force account, contracting, labour-based) the existing contacting capacity in the country and types and sizes of contrasts possible within the existing capacity, etc. Once this is done, a projection for the future should be done, with the following possible split of works in five to ten years:

○ Contracting   90%
○ Force account   10%

Classification of roadworks

A strategy should be established, based on a rational criteria, to classify works which need to be done under the following systems:

○ Equipment-based methods
○ Mix of equipment and labour
○ Labour-based methods.

Labour-based methods

Under the labour-based methods, which would include the MRP, an attempt should be made to move away from force account systems to contracting systems. For gravelling and regravelling by the use of labour-based contractors, the ongoing training of potential and interested people and firms in labour-based contracting should continue in order to provide the country with a good number of labour-based contractors who can bid for the works without creating cartels.

For routine maintenance works it would be important to start modifying the lengthman system of contracting, whereby each person works for two or three days per week on about 1.5km of road, to a system where petty contractors would bid for road lengths of up to 200km each. Training of petty contractors is, of course, necessary, and these would be the existing small road contractors, personnel leaving the public service or other interested people. As mentioned earlier, development of routine maintenance contracting systems and a training programme, including training materials, are necessary.

Financing

Although the government, with donor assistance, may be able to allocate the necessary resources to undertake the training, and also to allocate work to qualifying labour-based contractors, the lack of an institution to equip the contractors with the necessary tools and equipment may be a constraint on the development of labour-based contacting.

Setting up a construction bank through multilateral and bilateral donor assistance, and involving the government, would be the most feasible way to assist upcoming local contractors in the country. The bank would have a technical department which would work out how assistance would be given to the contractors. In this regard, a very close link between the bank, the client (MOPW&H) and the contractors would be necessary.

CHAPTER 9

Transformation of the Labour Construction Unit from an executing agency to a contract supervisory agency

A. Lehobo

Introduction

The Government of Lesotho established the Labour Construction Unit (LCU) in 1977 to counteract an impending massive repatriation of Basotho migrant labour from the Republic of South Africa. The long-term objectives of the LCU were to promote and propagate the use of efficient labour-intensive methods of construction in all public works, and to create as much gainful employment as possible in the country, especially for the returning migrant workers.

In 1988 the LCU became a full branch of the Ministry of Works with responsibility for maintenance, rehabilitation, upgrading and new construction of a rural road network of about 2300 kilometres. About 30 per cent of this road network was gravel roads in a maintainable state and about 70 per cent comprised earth roads to be upgraded to gravel standard and important tracks which required new construction. This responsibility for road constituted the bulk of the LCU's future operations and provided the means within which to develop the new branch of the Ministry of Works fully. The primary objectives of the LCU were then changed to the provision of a functional rural road communication system to improve the socio-economic conditions of rural people.

With SIDA financial assistance, a long-term (20 years) LCU Development Plan was prepared by the ILO consultants in 1989. The plan presented a growing responsibility of road maintenance, rehabilitation, upgrading and new construction until the year 2008, when all of the 2300km would be under routine and periodic maintenance (regravelling).

In line with the government policy of promoting private sector enterprises, the LCU began to explore possibilities of using local contractors to reduce the projected government establishment due to the increased work-load, and to enhance LCU operational efficiency. The immediate problem that confronted the LCU was the lack of indigenous contractors capable of implementing labour-based road maintenance. The Lesotho construction industry was dominated by foreign firms and non-indigenous locally-based contractors. The only available indigenous contractors were builders. These were poorly capitalized and lacked essential managerial and business skills. This implied the need for considerable initial support to train indigenous contractors to achieve a sustainable development of the construction industry in Lesotho, and a gradual transformation of the LCU into a client organization responsible for planning, design, contract award and supervision, leaving the implementation to contractors.

The LCU approached SIDA to finance a short study aimed at assessing the training needs of indigenous contractors and to determine the viability of a project for developing labour-based road maintenance contractors. The ILO carried out the study, whose final output was a detailed project document which the LCU submitted to World Bank and successfully negotiated funding for the project during May 1992.

Project profile

The World Bank financed the LCU contractor development project to the extent of US$3.4 million, a significant portion of the proceeds of IDA Credit No. 2400 LSO. As the client, the LCU retained overall responsibility for implementing the project, and commissioned the ILO under Agreement LES/92/02/IDA for the provision of consultancy services to the project. The name of the project, Enterpreneurship Development for Labour-Based Road Maintenance Contractors, evolved during project formulation stage. The alternative name of Small-Scale Contractors Project (SSCP) evolved during the implementation stage. The primary objectives of the project were:

○ the establishment of a local capacity among domestic small-scale contractors capable of undertaking labour-based road maintenance
○ the establishment of a system of administrational and financial procedures allowing labour-based contractors to compete for and execute public works contracts.

Development of contractors

Selection of trainees
It was against the background of non-availability of indigenous civil works contractors and the poor status of building contractors that the LCU considered three alternative sources of recruitment of contractors for training. These were building contractors, suppliers of haulage equipment, and LCU field staff at the level of senior technical officers and technical officers.

In order to qualify for training, applicants from these three sources were required:

○ to possess basic technical, management and business skills,
○ to have a bank account, and
○ to have some fixed assets.

Annexe 1 is an improved recruitment procedure adapted by the project and Annexe 2 shows the profile of contractors before training. The profile of contractors after training has not been provided in this paper but the developmental changes that occurred during training may be summarized as follows:

○ Contractors were active members of a newly-established Association of Road Maintenance and Construction Contractors.
○ All had acquired sufficient technical, management and business skills to undertake labour-based road maintenance contracts.
○ All had opened active business accounts with Lesotho Bank, and were credit-worthy.
○ Annual turnover/income for contractors had significantly increased.
○ All contractors had acquired additional handtools, and some of the contractors had bought second hand equipment pending the arrival of new project equipment.

Training programme

The training programme was designed to provide the integrated technical, management and business skills essential for labour-based road maintenance contractors. The programme consisted of classroom training, field training and trial contracts. Annexe 3 is the revised training programme as at February 1994. During classroom training participants were taught:

○ techniques of road maintenance using labour-based methods. Road maintenance and regravelling (ROMAR) training material was used for this purpose.
○ management and business skills using Improve Your Construction Business (IYCB) training material
○ contract documents in order to familiarize trainees with contract documents to be used during trial contracts and thereafter.

Lecturers were a mix of local and international consultants, ILO project staff, LCU training staff and guests invited from the Ministry of Labour, insurance companies and financial institutions in Lesotho.

The field training sessions combined demonstrations by contracts supervisors, and hands-on experience by trainees. The objective of this stage was to expose all trainees to all possible routine maintenance activities, including how each activity was planned and implemented, paying attention to the quality of handtools and labour productivity.

The three-month trial contracts were aimed at developing individual trainees' capacity to apply labour-based techniques to road maintenance. The trainees put into practice what they learnt during classroom and field training sessions. Each trainee learnt how to plan and organize his site in accordance with the contract and good business management. Strong emphasis was placed on the work techniques, the required work standards, labour productivity and equipment inputs. In fact, the trial contracts were life experience for trainees as future entrepreneurs. A majority of trainees made a good profit from the trial contracts.

Annexe 4 is the summary of the standard contracts for Routine Maintenance and Periodic Maintenance (Regravelling) which the LCU awarded to Batch 1 contractors. These contracts were planned, organized and supervised by the LCU operations section.

Training assessments

In order to ensure that the objectives of the contractor training project were being achieved two consultants, at different times, were commissioned to review the project with respect to training material, course duration and training approach. The following were the recommendations of the consultants:

○ selection of trainees to be improved to get a more homogeneous group
○ ROMAR training material to be substantially revised and modified along the same lines of IYCB, and those elements of the IYCB training material required by trainees to be rewritten to relate fully to road works
○ review of contract documents and the inclusion of one week of lectures on contract documents to be added to in the training programme
○ postponement of the second course to allow time for revision of training material, improvement of recruitment procedures and recruitment of contractors for the second course, in accordance with improved procedures.

Creation of an enabling environment

The project aimed at creating an enabling environment for the survival and development of small-scale contractors by addressing the following problems:

○ future market to provide contractors with continuous work to enable them to sustain an acceptable level of skilled personnel and other resources
○ contract documentation with restrictive tendering and contract requirements, such as provision of sureties
○ financial resources to purchase materials and tools, hire plant and pay wages for labour
○ training opportunities to equip contractors with technical, managerial and business skills.

Future market for contractors

The LCU long-term (20 year) development plan was found to be an adequate future market for trained labour-based contractors. The LCU proposed a work programme for funding by the World Bank under the recently appraised Road Rehabilitation and Maintenance Project (RRMP) scheduled for commencement during July 1995. The programme shows various types of road works and numbers of required contractors.

Contract documentation

The contract documents used by the project were simplified and adapted to labour-based road maintenance. Simplified as they might have been, the documents were comprehensive and they familiarized trainees with standard contract documents used in the Lesotho construction industry. Therefore the trainee contractors were afforded an opportunity for upward mobility within the construction industry through the use of contract documentation compatible with the standards prevailing in the construction industry.

The contract document for routine maintenance was only 23 pages long. There were two separate documents for regravelling contracts. These were the tender document and the contract document and they had the following in common: general and special conditions of contract, works specifications, bills of quantities (unpriced in the tender document and priced in the contract document), and drawings. The main features of the tender document were conditions of tender and instructions to tenderers.

The contract award procedure adopted by the project was as follows:

Road maintenance trial contracts
a. Select roads, produce contract lots of 10-15 km long for each contractor and prepare engineer's cost estimate for all contract lots equal to the number of trainees.
b. Inform the Central Tender Board (CTB) and seek the board's approval to use trainees to carry out routine maintenance on the selected roads, giving details of the proposed contract lots.
c. Call trainees to a meeting where contract lots are awarded through a ballot system agreed upon by the CTB and the LCU.

There was no tendering, and the engineer's estimate became the contract price.

Regravelling trial contracts
Steps a, b, and c for road maintenance trial contracts were carried out in the same order, and were then followed by:

d. Trainees prepared bids on their individual contract lots.

e. Bids were received by CTB, opened in public and returned to the LCU for evaluation by the project team. Bids within + 5 per cent of the engineer's cost estimate were recommended to CTB as good for execution of the contract, otherwise the engineer's cost estimates were recommended.

f. CTB approved the recommendations and the LCU awarded the contracts.

All field training activities and trial contracts were organized and closely supervised by the two project contracts supervisors. The contracts manager, or chief technical adviser (CTA), provided overall project co-ordination.

For routine maintenance contracts, monthly instructions were given to contractors by the supervisors. Instructions related to activities to be performed during the month. At the end of the month the contractor was either paid the full monthly lump sum as stated in the contract or paid a percentage of the monthly lump sum corresponding to the percentage of completed tasks.

In the case of regravelling contracts there were two alternative methods of payment. Alternative 1 involved measuring every item of completed work. The measured quantities of work were priced using unit cost rates in the priced bill of quantities. Alternative 2 was measuring the length of the regravelled portion of the contract length of the road which had been completed satisfactorily in all respects, and had passed compaction test, field dry density at 95 per cent or higher of laboratory maximum dry density. The measured length represented a percentage of total contract length upon which contract price was based. This percentage was then applied to the contract price to calculate the value of work done in the month.

Financial assistance

Except for a non-refundable admission fee of M300 (M = Maloti, US1$ = 3.6 M and 1 M = 1 Rand (Nov. 1995)), the trainee contractors went through a twelve-month course which equipped them with technical, managerial and business skills at no cost to them. All training costs for food, accommodation, transport salaries of lecturers and support staff, tools, etc. were paid for by the project.

During the trial contracts the trainees were given an opportunity to make money. Unit cost rates used in the calculation of the engineer's estimate for each trial contract included 7.5 per cent of total inputs for profit. Close supervision assisted trainees to improve their labour productivity rates which resulted in substantial savings on person-days and an increased profit margin for the contractors.

Trainee contractors received money in advance. For routine maintenance trial contracts, trainees were advanced with full amounts of wages for labour plus M500 as a monthly allowance/salary for the trainees, and 10 per cent of total wages to meet the contractor's expenses. The project recovered the money advanced to contractors by making deductions from monthly certificates. In the case of regravelling trial contracts, trainees received an advance of 20 per cent of the contract sum to enable them to open business accounts with the Lesotho Bank, to obtain bank guarantees, to buy additional tools and to pay wages for labour. The Lesotho Bank opened a current account with an overdraft facility for each trainee. The amount of overdraft was not allowed to exceed the available funds in the trainee's deposition/call account, or the value of the monthly payment certificate undergoing payment process, where copies of certificates were submitted to the bank by trainees.

Provision of tools and equipment

The project procured a sufficient number of handtools for routine maintenance trial contracts. The ownership of these handtools was transferred to the trainees, who in turn paid back the cost of the tools in monthly instalments during the period of trial contracts. Below is a list of handtools that were found adequate for the execution of routine maintenance activities on a 12 km road.

Regravelling trial contracts required more handtools and equipment for supply of water (tractor and water bowser), haulage of gravel (tipper or a combination of tractor and trailer), and compaction of gravel (pedestrian roller). Normally one tipper, two tractors and two trailers, two water bowsers and one supervision vehicle were more than adequate for the execution of a trial regravelling contract.

A majority of trainees owned supervision vehicles and they were able to make arrangements for the hire of tippers, tractors and trailers because these were easily available at commercial hire rates. Rollers and water bowsers were not readily available. Therefore the project procured 20 Dynapac pedestrian rollers and 11 water bowsers (1000 litres) for use by the contractors. Ownership of the rollers was transferred from the LCU to individual contractors

Table 9.1: Handtools for routine maintenance activities on 12 km road

Handtool	Quantity	Unit cost (Maloti)	Total cost (Maloti)
Wheelbarrow	8	145.00	1160.00
Pickaxe and handle	8	44.50	356.00
Shovel	8	54.00	432.00
Heavy-duty rake	8	36.50	292.00
Hand rammer	2	29.00	58.00
Sub total			2298.00
Add 5 per cent for LCU store handling charges			114.90
Total (Maloti)			2412.90
Total US$			670.25

through a lease financing agreement with the Lesotho Bank, and a hire-purchase agreement with the Agricultural Development Bank.

Due to the delayed procurement of rollers, Batch 1 trainees suffered during regravelling trial contracts. It was not easy for all of them to get rollers in the market. Available equipment often broke down, thereby causing serious delays and subsequent contract extension.

Development of client organization

This section reviews the current status of the LCU with respect to its transformation from an executing to a contract supervisory agency. The following issues are considered:

○ the capacity to supervise and administer contracts
○ arrangements to build the capacity to supervise and administer contracts.

Capacity to supervise and administer contracts

The LCU had built little capacity to supervise and administer contracts during the 30-month period of the entrepreneurship development project. However, this does not mean that the project has not achieved its immediate objective of providing the LCU with trained contractors. Indeed the project has produced accredited contractors in excess of project targets. The project strategy assumed that the LCU would build the required capacity as the project progressed through the successful integration of force account and contract works. Apparently the rate at which capacity was built was very slow. The author attributes the following factors as major causes:

○ failure to orientate the LCU staff towards its new role
○ failure to have a functioning project steering committee
○ the staffing situation at regional level
○ a change in the senior management in the LCU

Orientation of the LCU staff

With the exception of the training staff at the LCU training centre in Teyateyaneng, six technicians who trained together with contractors and three new engineers, none of the more than 250 members of the LCU staff received any formal orientation about the planned contracting-out of the LCU activities of routine road maintenance and road regravelling, and the eventual phasing-out of force account operations. Therefore the expected change in the attitude of staff towards the new role of the LCU has not occurred.

Project steering committee

The project document and the letter of agreement between the LCU and the ILO both stipulated the establishment of a steering committee to be charged with responsibility for providing guidelines necessary for the LCU to make essential changes concerning its transformation from an executing to a contract supervisory agency. This committee was established at the commencement of the project but it never became functional. Therefore its very important work was never done.

Staging situation at regional level

From the commencement of the project, the LCU began to receive engineers returning from training in the United Kingdom. These young engineers became regional engineers despite their limited experience. They were not formally or properly given orientation about the LCU entrepreneurship development project, but they were given responsibility for supervision and administration of both force account and contract works without any guidance to achieve the expected integration of the two operations. Of course, the project strategy did not provide any guidelines to achieve the expected integration. Therefore, with inexperienced staff that was not knowledgeable about contract management, small progress was achieved.

Changes in the senior management positions

The chief engineer (CE) and senior planning and control engineer (SPCE), who had both been very instrumental during the project formulation and planning stages, left the LCU as the project entered the implementation stage. These officers' contracts had expired and they were replaced by new incumbents from outside the LCU. Needless to say, these new officers learnt about the policies, objectives and operations of the LCU, including the entrepreneurship development for labour-based road maintenance contractors, from scratch. Therefore the momentum the project had gained was somewhat impeded. Worse still, the SPCE created a lot of misunderstandings about the project and the involvement of the ILO which, at one stage, led to much confusion and the ILO was on the verge of cancelling the agreement and withdrawing its technical assistance from the LCU entrepreneurship development project.

Arrangement to build capacity to supervise and administer contracts

In the recent document entitled *Training for small-scale contractors: Training of LCU staff and contract management*, which the LCU has submitted to the World Bank for financing under the road rehabilitation and maintenance project (RRMP), the LCU has expressed in detail its two most important requirements to implement the five year investment programme successfully. These two most important requirements are:

1. The establishment of a functional contracts section. The establishment of a contracts section was stipulated in the project document and the letter of agreement between the ILO and the LCU, but this has been delayed because of a lack of engineers to man the section. However, the LCU made a move

during 1994/95 when the organization received new engineers coming back from training in the United Kingdom. This move placed one of the new engineers in each of the two existing regions to deal specifically with contract work and a third engineer as counterpart to the contracts manager. Now the LCU intends to place a senior contracts engineer (SCE) as the head of the section in Maseru at the headquarters of the LCU, and one contracts engineer in each of the two existing regions. The SCE and his team will be mandated to build up the requisite capacity to handle contract work. This team will work closely with the regional engineers to achieve integration of the force account and contract works. Since the SCE and the two contracts engineers are likely to be expatriates, the LCU will provide counterparts and understudies.

2. The training of LCU engineers and technicians in contract management in order to man positions in the contracts section and to meet future contract demands of the LCU.

The LCU does not intend to involve consultants in its contract work to assist in the capacity-building and transition to its new role. This is clearly stated in *Training for small-scale contractors*. However, the organization intends to involve both local and international consultants in the extended entrepreneurship development programme, which will eventually include road construction and rehabilitation (ROCAR).

Lessons learnt and recommendations

Lessons
1. The LCU change of role over the 30 months of the project was insignificant because the project planning strategy provided a framework only for project execution, objectives, monitoring and control processes, and omitted:

   ○ analysis of the LCU resources to determine organizational strengths and weaknesses and the extent of change required from an executing to a contract supervisory agency
   ○ identification and evaluation of alternative project strategic approaches and providing the selected approach with clear step-by-step implementation guidelines in order to achieve the desired change of role.

2. The selection procedure for recruitment of trainees should aim at securing a homogeneous group to facilitate good understanding of all the components of the training programme. Batch I trainees, selected by the LCU, were a non-homogeneous group, whereas Batch 2 trainees were a homoge-

neous group recruited after a significant improvement in the selection procedure.

3. All training material must be complete, at least in final draft, before commencement of the training course; and it must be relevant to the training needs of the course participants. Due to a hiatus over the starting date of the project and insufficient preparatory time or resources being available, most of the technical road maintenance and regravelling (ROMAR) training material was unprepared when the course started. The Improve Your Construction Business (IYCB) business-oriented training material was also felt to be irrelevant to the needs of contractors for roadworks. Batch I trainees, some of them with no experience of building construction, were confused and found it difficult to relate IYCB building construction examples to roadworks. Significant improvements were made in the training material before and during the second course, Batch 2.

4. The project benefited from a rich mix of local and international consultants, who complemented each other with their respective specialized knowledge of local scene and international broad-based expertise. Involvement of local consultants and LCU training staff significantly improved the sustainability of local capacity to deliver ROMAR and IYCB training material in the future courses.

5. Intermittent project reviews built into the training programme were very useful and provided essential guidance, which led to the success of the two training courses – with an output in excess of project targets.

6. The overall training approach, a harmonized mix of classroom training, extensively supervised practical work comprising demonstrations and hands-on experience and trial contracts, gave trainees an excellent opportunity to acquire the requisite technical, managerial and business skills.

7. The project strategy of inviting senior representatives of financial institutions and insurance companies as guest lecturers facilitated an early interaction of trainees with these organizations and led to a mutual understanding of the requirements of all parties in order for the trainees to obtain access to credit facilities with ease.

8. The simplified yet comprehensive contract documentation adopted by the project provided the trainees with an opportunity to become familiar with existing standard tender and contract documents used in construction industry contracts elsewhere in the country.

Recommendations

1. Lessons learned from the LCU project serve as a list of recommendations to those public and private organizations intending to undertake a similar

project. Lessons with positive impact should be adapted with some modifications to suit local conditions, while lessons with negative impact should be avoided through the formulation of better project strategic plans.

2. With respect to the LCU, the following is recommended:

○ The project steering committee should be resuscitated to extend the contractor training programme.

○ The following outstanding project activities, as listed in the letter of agreement between LCU and the ILO, should be undertaken as a matter of urgency in order to expedite the transformation of the LCU to a client role and to facilitate smooth implementation of the five year investment programme by contractors:

a. All LCU staff (TA and above) should attend an introductory course (1-2 days) on the principles of contractor-executed projects and the implications for the LCU and its staff.

b. Guidelines should be developed for a road construction and rehabilitation (ROCAR) enterprise management package, drawing upon the experience of the introduction of the ROMAR package.

c. There should be a review of the LCU organization concerning its abilities to handle the introduction of private contractor-executed projects and the development of guidelines covering changes necessary.

As proposed by Derek Miles in his ROCAR strategy note, a strategic study is required to undertake activities b and c, and other issues of concern.

Bibliography

1. Quarterly Reports, Enterpreneurship Development for Labour-based Road Maintenance Contractors, LES/92/02/IDA.

2. Project Document, Entrepreneurship Development For Labour-based Road Maintenance Contractors.

3. Letter of Agreement, between the Government of Lesotho and ILO for Services to be Provided by ILO in Respect of Project Financed from IDA Credit to the Government by the World Bank.

4. Derek Miles, Entrepreneurship Development for Labour-based Road Maintenance Contractors: ROCAR Strategy Note, ILO, Geneva, 1995 (unpublished).

5. E. Berentsen, 'Small Scale Contractor Training Programme in Lesotho', Regional Seminar on Labour Cased Roadworks, University of the Witwatersrand, January 1995.

6. Labour Construction Unit, 'Training for Small Scale Contractors, Training of LCU Staff and Contract Management', August 1995.

7. T. Lehobo, 'Status of Basotho Contractors in the Construction and Maintenance of Civil Works Projects', August 1994.
8. T. Lehobo, 'Development Strategy for Contracting-out Labour-based Road Maintenance Works', March 1995.
9. S. Selatile, 'Entrepreneurship Development for Labour-based Road Maintenance Contractors', Training Assessment Consultancy, Preliminary Report, December 1993.
10. Arne Engdahl, 'Entrepreneurship Development for Labour-based Road Maintenance Contractors', Training Mission, March 1994.
11. A Beusch, 'Entrepreneurship Development for Labour-based Road Maintenance Contractors', ROMAR Course Report, October 1994.
12. O. Asare, 'Contracts Supervision and Administration', March 1995.

Annexe 1

Selection procedures of trainees (future contractors)
- Advertise on radio and in local newspapers 2-4 Weeks
- Applications by firms and individuals 4-6 Weeks (60-80 candidates)
- Review and screen applicants 2-3 Weeks
- Workshop and test 1 Day (30 - 40 Shortlisted)
- Screen and review test results 1 - 2 Weeks
- Invitation for personal interview (14-16 Applicants)
- Verification of information and final selection 2 - 3 Weeks
- (Shortlisted) trainees pay non-refundable admission fee (12 Trainees)
- Twelve month's contractor course starts

Annexe 2: Profile of contractors before training (batch 1). Issues considered when selecting candidates for training

Name of applicant	Highest academic qualifications	Type of operation Individual	Type of operation Small firm	Experience in contract work	Level of knowledge Technical (roads)	Level of knowledge Manage-ment	Busi-ness	Financial status Type of bank a/c	Financial status Fixed assets	Other resources
Mocha Moruthoane	COSC		Water borehole drilling and hire of farm equipment (not legally registered)	Water borehole drilling and hire of farm equipment with annual income of M80,000.00	None	Fair	Good	Business	2 borehole drilling machines, 5 tractors, one truck (7 ton), filling station	1 mechanic 1 plumber 4-12 labourers
Molapo Seetsa	COSC plus certificate in building technology		Construction and maintenance of buildings (legally registered)	Building contracts with annual income of M100,000.00	None	Good	Fair	Business	2 pick-ups, 1 concrete vibrator, 1 compacting plate and 1 residential house valued M200,000.00	2 bricklayers 1 carpenter 10-30 labourers handtools
George Thokoa	JC plus vocational training		Electrical installations (legally registered)	Electrical installation contracts with annual turnover of more than M50,000.00	None	Fair	Fair	Business	1 pickup	1 foreman 3-8 labourers handtools
Sipho Masholuogu	Diploma in civil engineering		Building and civil works (not legally registered)	Sub-contracts of civil works with an annual turnover of more than M60,000.00	Fair	Fair	Fair	Business	7 ton truck, 2 pickups, 2 concrete mixers residential house worth M40,000.00	1 foreman, 1 driver, 1 carpenter 5-30 labourers handtools
Mopeli Seetsa	Diploma in civil engineering	Employed by various firms		Involved in design and build civil works contracts undertaken by his employer with annual income of M18,000.00	Good	Fair	None	Savings	1 pick-up	
Michael Molefe	A certificate in teaching		Manufacture contracts with an annual income of over M150,000.00	Building contracts with an annual income of over M150,000.00	None	Fair	Good	Business	1 tipper, 9 ton truck, 3 pickups, 4 cars, buildings worth M650,000.00	Up to 50 labourers 2 bricklayers 1 carpenters clerk

Annexe 2: Contractor's profile (continued)

Name of applicant	Highest academic qualifications	Type of operation		Experience in contract work	Level of knowledge		Business	Financial status		Other resources
		Individual	Small firm		Technical (roads)	Management		Type of bank a/c	Fixed assets	
Church Mafantiri	JC plus vocational training	Self employed		Building contracts with an annual income of M45,000.00	None	Fair	Poor	Savings	1 pickup, five roomed house worth M45,000.00	1 concrete mixer, scaffolding, handtools, 5-10 labourers
Tiro Khoe	STD 7 plus vocational training	Self employed		Building contracts with an annual income of M50,000.00	None	Fair	Poor	Savings	1 pickup, residential house worth M75,000.00	Handtools, 5-10 labourers
Mophethe Mophethe	JC	Self employed		Building and civil works contracts with an annual income of M45,000.00	Fair	Fair	Poor	Savings	1 pickup and house worth M18,000.00	Handtools 5-10 labourers
Edwin Papashane	COSC + vocational training		Construction and maintenance of buildings (legally registered)	Building contracts with an annual turnover of M150,000.00	None	Fair	Fair	Business	1 pickup 1 concrete mixer 1 generator	1 foreman 1 carpenter, handtools 5-10 labourers
Moses Nkofo	COSC	Self employed		Worked as a sub-contractor in construction and maintenance of buildings with annual income of M50,000.00	None	Fair	Fair	Business	2.5 ton truck, 1 pickup, 3 business houses valued M285,000.00	1 foreman 1 bricklayer 5-10 labourers handtools
Mahau Maphephe	JC + vocational training	Self employed		Maintenance of buildings with an annual income of M28,000	None	Fair	Fair	Business	2 pickups, 7 ton truck and welding machine	Handtools, 5-10 labourers General Cafe
Thuso Sepetla	JC + vocational training	Self employed		Maintenance of buildings with an annual income of M28,000.00	None	Fair	Poor	Savings	1 pickup	Handtools

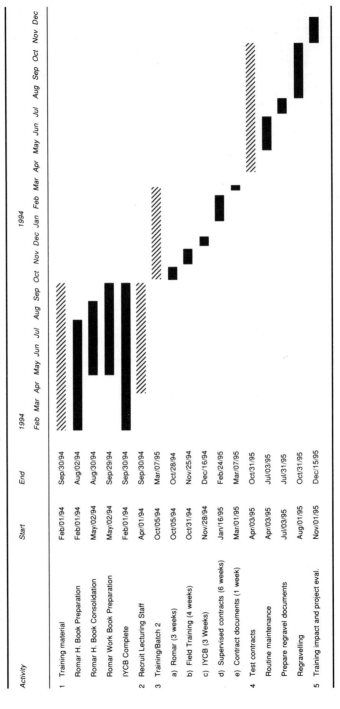

Annexe 3: Small scale contractors' training; revised programme, February 1994

Activity	Start	End
1 Training material	Feb/01/94	Sep/30/94
Romar H. Book Preparation	Feb/01/94	Aug/02/94
Romar H. Book Consolidation	May/02/94	Aug/30/94
Romar Work Book Preparation	May/02/94	Sep/29/94
IYCB Complete	Feb/01/94	Sep/30/94
2 Recruit Lecturing Staff	Apr/01/94	Sep/30/94
3 Training/Batch 2	Oct/05/94	Mar/07/95
a) Romar (3 weeks)	Oct/05/94	Oct/28/94
b) Field Training (4 weeks)	Oct/31/94	Nov/25/94
c) IYCB (3 Weeks)	Nov/28/94	Dec/16/94
d) Supervised contracts (6 weeks)	Jan/16/95	Feb/24/95
e) Contract documents (1 week)	Mar/01/95	Mar/07/95
4 Test contracts	Apr/03/95	Oct/31/95
Routine maintenance	Apr/03/95	Jul/03/95
Prepare regravel documents	Jul/03/95	Jul/31/95
Regravelling	Aug/01/95	Oct/31/95
5 Training impact and project eval.	Nov/01/95	Dec/15/95

Milestone △

Summary

Fixed delay ......

92

Annexe 4: Summary of standard contracts awarded to batch 1 trainees after completion of the course

Name of contractor	Routine maintenance			Regravelling contracts			
	Length km	Value Maloti	Duration months	Length km	Value Maloti	Duration (months) Planned	Actual
M Molefe				11	590 890	11	10
M Seetsa				10	599 233	9	10*
T Khooe				10	554 868	11	12*
M Nkofo				11	663 586	11	8
M Maphephe	34	171 228	12				
T Sepetla	30	157 692	12				
C Manfantiri	34	170 808	12				
G Thokoa	32	173 976	12				
M Moruthoane	31	163 056	12				
M Mophethe	35	186 360	12				
M Seetsa	36	189 264	12				
E Papashane	33	166 416	12				
Totals (Maloti)		1 378 880			2 408 577		
Totals (US $)		383 000			669 049		

Notes

1. Exchange rate US $1 = M 3.6 (Nov 1995).
2. Four regravelling contracts awarded through competitive bidding by eight contractors qualified for this category of contract.
3. Routine maintenance contracts were awarded through a ballot system. There was no tendering; the contract value was the engineer's estimate for each road.
4. *Contract is on-going; completion time is a forecast.

1 M = Maloti US 1$ = 3.6 M and 1 M = 1 Rand (Nov. 1995)

CHAPTER 10

Road maintenance using local small-scale contractors

W. Musumba

Introduction

Since 1986 the Government of Uganda has reconstructed or rehabilitated over 50 per cent of the main roads and 20 per cent of the feeder roads at a total cost of about US$300 million. There was therefore mounting pressure to protect this enormous investment. In 1992 under the auspices of the road maintenance initiative an in-depth analysis of problems related to road maintenance was undertaken. This led to the formulation of revised policies and strategies which now form the basis under which the contracting option was adopted. The government's medium-term highway network policy is the following:

○ the provision of an efficient, safe and sustainable main roads network as a support for accelerated integrated development and consolidation of peace and national unity
○ the development of the local construction industry as a measure of ensuring a sustainable road network.

The road maintenance strategies that have been adopted are presented in Annexe 1. The government undertook a deliberate policy to increase the use of the contracting option, and under the ongoing four-year road maintenance programme (MRMP). The targets shown in Table 10.1 were set.

It was, however, noted that the local contracting industry was ill equipped and could develop only gradually through affirmative action by government.

Table 10.1:

	94/95	95/96	96/97	97/98
Private sector share of maintenance works (%)	40	50	65	80

Further experience had shown that potential small-scale contractors lacked experience in quoting, hence it became extremely difficult for them to break into the market. The adoption of fixed unit rates was therefore found to be the most feasible approach.

This paper discusses the labour-based contracting programme (LBCP) and the fixed unit rate mechanized maintenance programme (FURMMP) of works, transport and communications under the feeder roads project managed by the Ministry of Local Government (MOLG). The objective of the contracting initiatives is to develop the local contracting industry's sustainable capacity for road works using small-scale contractors.

The labour-based contracting programme (LBCP)

This programme has been in operation since January 1993.

Policy direction

The Ministry of Works, Transport and Communications policy is to use private contractors increasingly due to the cost effectiveness and increased efficiency of operations. The old policy, which was highly dependent on force account operations, had several constraints which the increased use of contractors aims to reduce.

Project data

The labour-based contracting programme (LBCP) is financed entirely by the Government of Uganda. Its 1995/96 budget of US$3.2 million is financed from the 1995/96 main road maintenance programme budget of US$17 million. The annual turnover for a typical lengthman contractor (Maintenance of 2km) currently stands at US$360. The LBCP is a routine activity budgeted for annually under the road maintenance recurrent budget.

Planning the programme

Any successful programme requires adequate planning. The main preparatory period lasted a year, January to December 1992, during which the following were carried out.

○ An appropriate road maintenance management manual was developed. It included guidelines on the implementation and management of labour-based contracts for routine manual maintenance through the respective local councils.

○ Public awareness programmes were undertaken on radio, television, paper media and contacts with the general public.

○ A workshop jointly organized by the Ministry of Works, Transport and Communications (MOWTC), the Ministry of Local Government (MOLG) and the International Labour Office (ILO) on the utilization of labour-

based methods of road maintenance was held in September 1992. This workshop fully endorsed the labour-based technology and marked the beginning of an organized and focused approach to the technology.
○ Road maintenance project accounts were opened in all the MOWTC districts.

Project activities

The programme targets all the manual routine maintenance activities which are normally carried out on both paved and unpaved (gravel) roads. The list of activities includes the removal of obstructions, drainage repairs, filling of potholes and rubbing (for unpaved roads only), vegetation control and tree planting.

Work methods for the different activities have been standardized and specifications issued.

Procurement of contractors

Contracts are let out on a yearly basis for each financial year (July-June). The following methodology has been adopted:

○ Lengthman contracts of 2km and group contracts of 10km each.
○ Application forms are available at the nearest MOWTC station, to which completed forms are also returned. A typical prequalification form is shown in Annexe 2.
○ To ensure that the contracts are availed to the people within a particular vicinity, all applicants are recommended by the chairman of their respective Resistance Council III (sub-country level).
○ Selection is carried out by the district engineers (MOWTC), based on the rating criteria shown in Table 10.2.

The best ranked contractor is awarded the contract.

○ Participation is open both to men and women; and considerable effort has been taken to encourage women to take up these contracts

Table 10.2:

Criterion	Rating
Experience in roadworks	3
Resistance Council III (chairman confirmation)	1
Address	1
Tools available (inspection)	2
Personnel (inspected)	1
Supervisory transport (bicycle)	1
Reputation	1
Total	**10**

○ The type of contracts adopted are fixed rate contracts, whose rates are determined annually after a countywide market rate survey before approval by the central tender board.
○ To ensure job continuity throughout the year for contractors the workload for the various activities has been spread out evenly. However, seasonal variations and applicable frequencies for the various activities are taken into account.

Supervision

The supervision of the contractors is carried out by the district engineer with a team of engineering assistants and road inspectors/overseers, who are each assigned to a particular section of road. The supervisory role includes giving planned working instructions to contractors, inspection during execution, work evaluation and measurement, training and so on.

The measurement of work is carried out once a month during an end-of-month inspection, together with the contractor. The final work measurement is counter signed by the contractor and the month's payment is based on it. Payment is by cheque signed by both the district engineer (DE) and the district executive secretary (DES). The payments are decentralized to DE level and are effected from project accounts which ensures prompt payments to contractors.

Tools

Initially tools were provided for the contractors. However, contractors are currently responsible for provision of their own tools, which are readily available. The Ministry still provides expensive tools, such as wheelbarrows, to interested contractors.

Contract documents

Every successful applicant for a maintenance contract signs an agreement with the Ministry (MOWTC), which the district engineer countersigns on behalf of the Ministry of Works, Transport and Communications.

The contract documents, which were 'tailor-made' for this programme, are small and simple and consist of the following:

1. Form of Agreement with five articles, namely:

    ○ obligations of contractors
    ○ obligations of the Ministry
    ○ contract price and mode of payment
    ○ commencement, duration and termination
    ○ modification, and settlement of disputes.

2. Bill of quantities
3. Specifications

4. Work plan

The contract is signed between the DE, with the DES as his witness, on one hand and the lengthman or group leader, with his witness, on the other. The contract is available as a separate document.

Organization
MOWTC was originally carrying out its work using force account units. It was found necessary to establish a separate unit within the organization structures to be explicitly responsible for contracting works.

Measurements
The evaluation for the work carried out by the contractor is done at the end of every month during an end-of-month inspection. This inspection is carried out by the DE, the particular supervisor, and the contractor to evaluate the progress in executing the monthly work-plan. The measurement of the progress is taken and the measurement sheet is signed jointly by the team, and thereafter is used for processing payment. Initially two options were left to the DE in effecting progress evaluation work:

○ Option 1. Assessment by percentage of work done, with a corresponding payment of the same percentage of the maximum payable.
○ Option 2. Measure the executed work and use approved unit rates to determine the actual payment due to the contractor.

Experience showed that option 1 was highly subjective and was open to abuse. Option 2 (taking actual measurements) was finally adopted.

Payment arrangements
The programme is funded entirely by the Government of Uganda, which makes advance payments to the decentralized accounts, ensuring prompt payments to the contractors.

Expansion of the programme
The expansion of the programme has had the following results:

Table 10.3:

Year	km	Cost US $ million
92/93	2500	0.7
93/94	5500	1.7
94/95	7500	2.0
95/96	8832	3.2

Table 10.4:

Management levels	Training requirements
Level 1: HQ, Regions Policies Decisions	Awareness creation Management
Level 2 : District Planning Supervision	Practice-oriented training
Level 3 : Site Planning Supervision	Practice-oriented training
Level 4 : Contractor Implementation	On-the-job training

Training

Training has been mainly on-the-job. However, a number of workshops and short courses have been held for DEs and supervisors. These training sessions are in addition to the 'all-together approach' that brought all the DEs together for quarterly meetings and seminars at the conception and planning phase of programme.

A comprehensive training programme (available as a separate document) has been started but only on a limited scale. The principal training requirements for the MOWTC routine maintenance organization is summarized in Table 10.4.

It is proposed to carry out decentralized training that will cover all personnel involved in the implementation of the programme. While the Ugandan Government is in a position to finance the local costs, the central project cost of US$172 000 is still outstanding, and includes:

○ international consultancy to prepare the training materials, set up the first course, monitor and design follow-up
○ preparing the contractor handbook
○ seconding local expert instructors
○ conducting initial courses, inclusive of training materials, allowances, accommodation, etc. While the labour-based contracting programme is operating satisfactorily, the training component is still a key requirement.

Experiences of the programme

The actual output, station by station, ranges from 60 per cent to 90 per cent. Some notable experiences of the programme include:

○ *Maintainable status.* The roads have reverted to a maintainable status. Additionally, intervention by mechanical means is used as and when the need arises.

○ *Training programmes.* The training component is still a key requirement which needs to be addressed seriously for the programme to achieve its objectives.

○ *Unit costs.* Earlier attempts to obtain unit rates through competitive bidding resulted in excessively high rates. For this programme, the Ministry worked out appropriate unit rates which are reviewed periodically, as and when there is a need. These rates are based on the current daily market rates.

○ *Tools.* Funds budgeted in the programme should provide tools to ensure availability and quality.

○ *Contractors.* Although initially lengthman contractors had a better output, group contractors have picked up and there is now consideration to expand the contract limit from 10km to 20km.

○ *Target group.* This programme was targeted at the direct participation of people living in the rural communities along the roads. The Ministry implemented four categories of payment rates applicable to different areas in the country. Initially people from towns rushed in hoping to make large profits. The situation has levelled out, with the programme now more or less attracting the target group.

Future programme
The following matters will be addressed in the future programme.

○ The Government intends to enhance the training programme through the different road maintenance programmes that have started or are about to start, co-financed by IDA, EU, KFW, ODA and ADB.

○ The maximum scope for contractors is to be increased to 20 km in the 1996/97 and ultimately to 50km in the 1998/99 financial year.

○ The issue of supervisory transport is being addressed in the different maintenance programmes.

○ Following the completion of the restructuring of the MOWTC, recruitment of key staff (e.g. overseers and supervisors) is to be undertaken.

○ Small-scale contractors have been encouraged to form an association.

○ Planting of trees is to be encouraged.

Fixed unit rate mechanized contracting programme

Planning of the programme
This programme was started in October 1994 and has been ongoing since then.

Basis

According to the new maintenance strategies, all routine maintenance will ultimately (by the year 2000) be carried out by contract. Another strategy is aimed at capacity-building through developing local contractors. This programme was started to fulfil these two strategies.

Planning phase

The planning phase occurred during the period June to September 1994 when the following were carried out:

○ Unit rates were developed and approved by the central tender board. These were based on recent and ongoing contracts, and rationalization through the engineers' estimates.
○ Intending contractors were prequalified and placed in the classes shown in Table 10.5 by the Ministry and the central tender board:
○ Candidate roads were surveyed, leading to Bills of Quantities.
○ Special contract documents were developed.

Programme activities

This programme is targeted at developing contractors to carry out routine mechanized maintenance. Activities include grading, drainage repairs, spot regravelling on unpaved roads and pothole patching and shoulder repairs for paved roads.

Procurement of contractors

The chief road maintenance engineer selects the contractors on the basis of the prequalification and track record of bidding contractors. An offer is given to the selected contractor, and if the contractor accepts the offer a contract is signed between the contractor and the Ministry, represented by the engineer-in-chief.

Equipment

In an effort to offer affirmative support for the emerging contractors, MOWTC adopted a policy whereby contractors can now hire idle equipment. Those in

Table 10.5:

Class	Limit of contract (US $)	Number of prequalified contractors
A	150 000	9
B	100 000	24
C	50 000	19
D	20 000	14

a position to repair broken-down equipment can repair, hire and utilize the equipment for a given period to offset the repair costs.

Contract documents
Simplified contract documents were specially developed. FIDIC conditions of contract are still applicable with appropriate adjustments given through particular conditions of contracts.

Measurement
Supervision is carried out by the DE, and payment is made against actual work performed, measured by the DE and certified by the chief road maintenance engineer, and the finally engineer-in-chief.

Outcome of the programme
The programme, has been extremely successful. It has been used to maintain a total of 492km (123km paved and 369km unpaved) at a cost of about US$1.4 million. In the process nine contractors have been engaged, some of whom have shown good potential to develop. The outcome of the 1994/95 programme is illustrated in Table 10.6.

Improvements to the programme
The programme, which had a limited scope, was to be expanded for the maintenance of about 2000km in the 1995/96 maintenance programme. The unit rates have been reviewed and some articles that were missing from the current contract documents have now been included.

Feeder roads project

Policy direction
The policy direction of the Ministry of Local Government is more or less the same as that of Ministry of Works, Transport and Communications, but with different targets for attaining local contracting capacity. The Ministry has among its objectives the introduction of labour-based methods of road

Table 10.6:

Activity	Programmed quality	Achieved quality	Total cost US $ million
Pothole patching and shoulder repair	172	123.2	0.15
Light grading	273	273	0.80
Heavy grading (inc. spot regravelling)	96	96	0.45

maintenance and feeder roads rehabilitation, wherever they are more cost effective.

Project data
This is part of the feeder roads component of the transport rehabilitation project. It is financed by IDA, NDF and CRU. The value of the works is US$8.7m over a four-year period starting in 1995. The annual turnover for a typical contractor is in the range of US$240,000 for rehabilitation works of about 20 – 25 km.

Planning of the programme
This is a typical donor-supported project whose planning started way back in 1992, culminating in the launching of the project in January 1995.

Project activities
The relevant project activities include rehabilitation of 680km and maintenance of 880km of feeder roads in the four districts of Mbale, Kapchorwa, Tororo and Pallisa, Eastern Uganda. The project proposes to use labour-based methods in combination with light equipment, e.g. farm tractors, trailers, pickups, motorcycles, pedestrian rollers, etc.

Technical assistance has been provided to steer the programme. Notable in the technical assistance team are local expert staff.

Procurement of contractors
Interested contractors who apply after advertisement in the press are short-listed for training. Work is given to selected contractors who are successful in the training programmes.

Equipment
The project attempts to address the main constraint on contractors – the lack of equipment – by procuring the necessary equipment and tools. A financing/leasing company will be formed and will be responsible for the leasing of equipment. The leasing company will also be linked to a local bank which will handle payments and provide working capital to contractors. This leasing arrangement has been a highly motivating factor to the aspiring contractors.

Contract documents
The consultant is to produce appropriate contracting documents.

Training
The programme has an elaborate training programme which the consultant is currently finalizing. Broadly, the contractor-training will take the following form:

○ two weeks introduction on a construction demonstration site
○ four months of intensive training on selected sites
○ continuous training on maintenance activities.

Current status
The project is in its first year of operation, which will consist mainly of training.

Conclusion

Labour-based technology has been firmly accepted in Uganda by all parties concerned. The programme has been received with particular enthusiasm by the contractors. The labour-based approach offers much-needed extra income to the rural dwellers and evolves a sense of ownership resulting in a protective attitude towards the road structure.

The different levels of contracting that exist offer a chance for the contractor to develop gradually up to the level of local competitive bidding.

The Uganda programmes have a very high level of funding by the government which has increased gradually over the years. This augurs well for the sustainability of the small-scale contracting programmes. Indeed, the implementation of the already-declared government privatization programme will ensure more opportunities for the private contracting sector.

Bibliography

Road Maintenance Management Guidelines, August, 1993.

Four Year Main Road Maintenance Programme, June, 1994.

Four Year Main Road Maintenance Programme: First Annual Progress Report, April 1995.

Labour Based Contract Maintenance Programme: Orientation Course for District Engineers by Intech Beusch & Co., April, 1993.

MOWTC Works Contract (Labour Based)

Proposal for Contractor Training Support, MOWTC, Dec. 1993.

Transport Rehabilitation Project: Feeder Roads Component, Implementation Manual, Oct. 1994.

Strategy for Rural Feeder Roads Rehabilitation and Maintenance, March, 1992.

Annexe 1

Road maintenance strategies
In line with the road maintenance policy, the following progress on road maintenance strategies has been achieved.

Awareness campaign
○ awareness campaigns that commenced in 1990 are to continue.

Road maintenance financing and disbursements
○ a road maintenance fund operated outside the traditional government will be established
○ a study was instituted by GTZ; government is yet to take a firm decision on the recommendation to establish the fund
○ road maintenance project accounts were opened in all districts in the 1992/ 93 financial year.

Road maintenance operations
○ routine manual maintenance operations are executed through small labour contracts
○ mechanized routine maintenance operations will increasingly be undertaken by contract. Works of an emergency nature will be handled by force account units. These units will be task-oriented. Appropriate performance allowances have been introduced for these force account operation units.
○ periodic maintenance, rehabilitation and reconstruction works are undertaken by mechanized contractors.

Capacity building
○ plant hire pool: a study to determine the scope of investment and other modalities to do with its establishment and operation is currently in progress.
○ training: to address the acute shortage of technical and management skills in the local construction industry, vigorous training programmes have been mounted to ensure that by the end of 1998 the industry will be equipped with adequate numbers of technicians and managers. Practical training of plant operators and mechanics will be imparted by means of a training production unit (TPU) which has already been established.

Institutional reform
○ an autonomous road authority will be established. Prior to its establishment, a study to define the authority will be mounted, and appropriate legislation put in place. This study is dependent on a decision on the road fund yet to be taken by government, since a road fund is essential for a road authority.

Annexe 2

Ministry of works, transport and communications

Lengthman/labour group contracts prequalification form

Road link   from KM   to KM

1. Name of group leader/lengthman

2. Sex

3. Age

4. Village (RC 1)   Parish (RC II)   RC III

5. Previous experience in road maintenance.

6. List the names of your labour group, stating age and sex.
   Name   Sex   Age

7. List the road-maintenance hand tools that you have (hoes, shovels, axes, pangas, etc.)

8. Do you have a bank account? If so, which bank?

9. Signature of group leader/lengthman

10. Recommendation by the RC III Chairman

For official use only
11. Supervisor's remarks:

12. Action taken:

13. District engineer

14. District executive secretary

CHAPTER 11

An Afrocentric approach to small-scale contractor development in South Africa

J. Ward

The primary task of a development programme is to help the client system to increase its control of its environment (including the local physical environment and the external environment that comprises the wider socio-economic–political system). Eric Miller[1]

Background – a legacy of autocracy

During the late 1960s and early 1970s, South Africa's construction industry was decidedly Eurocentric. White contractors competed comfortably among themselves for most types of work within a relatively protected economy. Site supervision was, for the most part, carried out by 'old-style' white general foremen who were considered by their employers to be highly experienced in controlling the black labour force.[2] What did this mean in practice? The supervisory style utilized by these foremen was implicitly based upon what Douglas McGregor described as 'Theory X: the traditional view of direction and control'.

In practice it was often worse than the application of an outdated management theory, and the behaviour was frequently brutal and racialistic, although at that time it would have been considered by most contractors to be the norm. Whatever the ratio of foreman-brutality to output-achieved might have been,

---

Theory X

1. The average human being has inherent dislike of work and will avoid it if he can.

2. Because of this human characteristic of dislike of work, most people must be coerced, controlled, directed, threatened with punishment to get them to put forth adequate effort toward the achievement of organizational objectives.

3. The average human being prefers to be directed, wishes to avoid responsibility, has relatively little ambition, wants security above all.[3]

---

there was, in this apartheid-driven system of productivity management, a total lack of humanity in the methods employed for achieving maximum productivity from the workhorse.

Thus although South Africa has considerable assets in terms of technical skills and an impressive range of academic and professional institutions, it also has a good deal to learn from the post-colonial experience of other African countries. In these countries, partly as an outcome of successive aid programmes managed by organizations and individuals chosen for their commitment to a non-racial approach, construction managers from different racial backgrounds gradually came to learn that training and entrepreneurial development has to be adapted to suit the African environment. They also came to realize that the small-scale contractor is the backbone of the emergent Afrocentric construction industry. They understood that the requirement for the African contractor to adapt to a Eurocentric construction environment is not an option to be considered. In short, a more appropriate set of assumptions are those set out in McGregor's Theory Y.

A New South Africa was born in April 1993, and the anachronism of the 'old-style' general foreman is no more. In the New South Africa, knowledge gained in emergent Africa can help with the reconstruction and development of the construction industry, with particular emphasis on the small-scale sector. Construction professionals working in the non-racial developing countries on the African continent have learned a great deal about the Afrocentric construction environment – the environment in which the small-scale contractor must make his, or her, living. They have learned ways by which small-scale construction entrepreneurs can be assisted in their efforts to achieve success.

Although the corpse of apartheid has been nailed firmly into its coffin, its ghost still walks, and will continue to walk until the attitudes of the (predomi-

---

Theory Y

1. The expenditure of physical and mental effort in work is as natural as play or rest.

2. External control and the threat of punishment are not the only means for bringing about effort toward organizational objectives.

3. Commitment to objectives is a function of the rewards associated with their achievement.

4. The average human being learns, under proper conditions, not only to accept but to seek responsibility.

5. The capacity to exercise a relatively high degree of imagination, ingenuity, and creativity in the solution of organizational problems is widely, not narrowly, distributed in the population.

6. Under the conditions of modern industrial life, the intellectual potentialities of the average human being are only partially utilized.[4]

---

nantly white) senior management in the South African construction industry change. This is particularly true of the small-scale construction sector. The construction industry is still very much under their control. With few exceptions, the methodology used in the training of small-scale contractors too often smacks of the consequences of apartheid and isolationism on the construction sector. In principle, senior management may welcome contact with the rest of Africa. But the reality sometimes paints a darker picture of defensiveness bordering on xenophobia.

This paper, with its criticisms, suggestions, proposals and recommendations, has been prepared from information gained over a three-year period of living and working in the New South Africa following a developing involvement in contractor training as a training adviser on technical co-operation projects in Lesotho, Vanuatu and Ghana. It is based on formal and informal discussions with representatives from the various sectors and sub-sectors of the construction industry, although the opinions are my own.

Emerging into independence?

Under the apartheid regime the black contractor was constrained by racially biased restrictions to such an extent that normal development was impossible. Despite this despotic restriction of entrepreneurial spirit, the small-scale black contractor achieved some degree of emergence, particularly in the field of black-owned private housing developments within the restricting township boundaries. Another route of emergence was for a black contractor to become a sub-contractor to a white contractor, often a 'front man' (hardly ever a 'front woman'). This gave the African limited access to work in the white residential areas.[5]

It is therefore important to realize that, while all black contractors are described as being 'emergent', several hundred of them have been 'emerging' for up to 40 years. Many are, and always have been, contractors in their own right, who will take sub-contracts only when there is no alternative. It is also important to differentiate between small-scale contractors and sub-contractors, since the latter will inevitably continue to be dependent on main contractors. The aspirations of the majority of small-scale contractors are simple and easy to understand, and they can be readily summarized in one major anticipative statement: *Small-scale contractors wish to be independent operators*[6]

In order to achieve this goal they realize that they have a great need for certain aspects of construction management training. They wish to be able to compete with the white contractors, in all residential areas, in all sub-sectors, and at all times. Small-scale contractor training programmes must therefore contain a large element of confidence-building, until there is a realization that they are capable of standing on their own feet, not requiring hand-outs and patronage from white contractors in the form of poorly paid labour-only sub-contracts.[7]

Sub-contractors, on the other hand, have different aspirations, and consequently different training needs. Their immediate goal is to be employed at a reasonable rate of remuneration, usually task-based or piecework-oriented.[8] Although they may be describe themselves as being self-employed, they are controlled by superior management forces in the form of main contractor supervisors who control their productivity, main contractor stores personnel who control their material supplies; and main contractor site clerks who control their cash flow.

There is a very basic difference between the small-scale construction entrepreneur and the sub-contractor. The former will set the task in order to increase the productivity of the workforce and expect to profit from the application of this management skill. The latter will have the task set by the main contractor, with effective dependency since responsibility for key decisions – and the bulk of the resulting profit – goes to the main contractor. As its title implies, this paper is primarily concerned with developing contractors rather than sub-contractors.

Creating an enabling environment

The present Eurocentric construction environment should be altered in order to make it more enabling for the black contractor. In order to make this paradigm shift it is necessary to enumerate the ethnic and cultural differences that exist between black contractors and other racial groups operating in the South African construction industry.[9]

Listening banks – do they exist?

There is a strong feeling among small-scale black contractors that commercial banks always lend to white contractors, but seldom lend to black contractors.[10] While they understand the constraints under which the bank managers have to work when assessing loan applications, the small-scale black contractors are convinced that there exists an element of racial discrimination which influences the decision of the white bank manager.[11] Few, if any, current South African-based training courses for small-scale contractors adequately address the issue of acquiring financial backing.

Constrained by collateral

While the commercial banks prefer collateral to be of the 'bricks and mortar' kind, many small-scale contractors may own sizeable areas of land and/or small dwellings. White contractors would tend to be owners of larger, more substantial dwellings on comparatively small plots. During the apartheid era, the Group Areas Act effectively barred blacks from owning property in the more up-market areas favoured by the finance companies. African wealth is often measured in terms of cattle or other agricultural possessions, such as fruit trees, which are not acceptable as collateral. Ownership of a Mercedes-Benz is the current trend among the affluent.[12]

Earning authority
Authority is no longer automatically invested along with the possession of a white skin. It has to be earned. Africans invest their peers with authority for different reasons, such as age, experience, ability and self-control.

External influences
Pressures peculiar to the African environment must be taken into consideration. These include family and ethnic tribal loyalties, particularly where the extended family is concerned. They may also include involvement in politics.

Top-down training
Illiteracy is not a sign of lack of intelligence. Patience and effective communication skills are demanded of trainers. Training materials and methodologies that are condescending and patronizing towards the disadvantaged recipients are to be strongly discouraged, even condemned. Black contractors do not need to be over-protected. Most project-based methods of contractor training have training and development methodologies that cocoon contractors to such an extent that they have little opportunity to use their own initiative. This form of training has never been used in the past to develop small-scale white contractors, so why it should now be used to develop small-scale black contractors is an enigma. The fact that the majority of white trainers may not realize that their methods can be seen as patronizing, condescending and racialistic strengthens the case for the use of Afrocentric trainers and training materials.[13]

Inappropriate standards
'Colonial' standards are inappropriate. The European concept of what type of dwellings Africans choose to inhabit is often proved to be wrong. Urban dwellers do not, as a rule, choose to live in adobe *khayas*, plain cinder block houses with sheet roofs, or prefabricated buildings.[14]

To summarize, an Afrocentric enabling environment requires:

- easier access to bank finance
- different forms of collateral
- a revised mandate for the investing of authority
- cognizance made of external influences on contractors
- acceptance of individuals for training on the basis of experience rather than academic qualifications, and the use of an appropriate training methodology
- building and construction standards and specifications based on African ideals, not on European imports.

Appropriate training methodologies

Accomplishing a complete change in the business environment affecting the South African construction industry is sure to take a very long time, but that is no reason to delay the conceptual change required in the present training methodology. To do this, decision-makers must first acquire sufficient humility to learn from others. There are various management programmes and courses for small-scale contractor development that have been developed in Africa which could be readily adapted to suit the ethnic South African construction environment. This programme must have the endorsement, patronage, sponsorship and support of the South African Government for it to succeed.[15] In order to achieve this, existing parameters of accreditation should be widened. The pre-programme assessment of candidates for training should concentrate more on experience and less on academic ability; more on entrepreneurial flair and less on financial stability; more on aptitude and less on a stereotyped character.

Conclusions

A. The South African construction industry
In South Africa, the construction industry is predominantly in the hands of medium and large-scale enterprises which are mainly owned and controlled by the white sector of the population. It is therefore essential that any contractor development programme addresses the following key issues:

○ Redressing the previous political dispensation which favoured the creation of white-owned businesses, policies such as job reservation, disparities in education standards and associated funding levels between different population groups.
○ Refocusing the structure of training in the industry which has largely been aimed at improving skills in the technical field to produce quality workers/employees for major conventional contracting firms.
○ Recognizing that the small-scale sector of the construction industry is not only a significant source of direct employment, but is also a sector that contributes, through its wide range of operations and labour-based projects, to the growth and development of virtually all other sectors of the industry where labour-based methods are able to be adopted.
○ Meeting the overwhelming need for the provision of roads into, and infrastructure within, communities in order to serve those millions of people who have been disadvantaged for decades.
○ Focusing on the small-scale construction entrepreneurs, from both the formal and the informal sectors, who make up the largest percentage of contractors, and are in need of assistance to help them organize and develop their enterprises so that they may assume their rightful role and fulfil their potential in the labour-based sector. There is a vast need for the Afrocentric-oriented training of participants in the labour-based sector of the construction industry in South Africa, in order to ensure that it will be able to meet

the demands that will be placed upon it during the period of reconstruction and development.

B. Initiatives to support the growth of small-scale contractors

○ Contractor training should place a strong emphasis on confidence-building, in order to encourage independence among black small-scale contractors and counteract the ravages of apartheid.

○ Small-scale contractors should be encouraged to take more responsibility for contract management at an early stage.

○ A project management or development team should avoid exercising excessive control (materials purchase, task-setting and so on) over the contractor's legitimate operations and encourage an early exposure to the business environment.

○ Training advisers should differentiate between sub-contractors and small-scale contractors and adjust their training methodologies accordingly.

○ Training methodology linked to productivity on site must never be allowed to exploit small-scale contractors or sub-contractors.

○ Efforts should be made to encourage commercial banks to become more small contractor-friendly .

○ Trainers who are not ethnic Africans should attend training-of-trainer programmes which teach non-condescending and non-patronizing methods of communication with small-scale black contractors, sub-contractors and community contractors.

○ Training materials must be practical, with action exercises that call upon the contractors' site experience for a solution.

○ There should be a minimum of lecturing by trainers and a maximum of group work by participants.

○ Contract documents, specifications, designs and choice of building materials should be made more Afrocentric.

References

1. Miller, Eric (1993), *From Dependency to Autonomy: Studies in Organization and Change*, Free Association Books, London.
2. ILO (1994), 'Advisory Mission to COSA TU', Unpublished report dated 15 April 1994, ILO, Geneva.
3. McGregor, Douglas (1987), *The Human Side of Enterprise*, Penguin Business Library, London, pp.33-34.
4. McGregor, Douglas, *Op cit.* pp.47-48.
5. ILO (1994), *Op cit.*
6. Ward, J.(1995), 'Training and Development Needs of Small-scale Contractors Operating in the Durban Functional Region', Unpublished report, Khuphuka, Durban.

7. Statement by J. Mogale (President: African Builders' Association) in article by Knowler G. (1993), *Developing Black Builders to tackle the Housing Backlog*, Natal Mercury, Durban.
8. ILO (1994), *Op cit.*
9. Lourens, P.E. (1993), 'Reconstruction and Development of the Construction Industry: The Need for a Paradigm Shift', Unpublished paper dated 29 June 1993, NABCAT, Johannesburg.
10. Ward, J. (1995), *Op cit.*
11. Sapere, D. (1993), 'Local Technology: A Tool for Informal Sector-driven Change', Unpublished paper dated 29 June 1993, NABCAT, Johannesburg.
12. Sapere D. (1993), *Op cit.*
13. National Public Works Programme (NPWP), Second Draft of Report by the Vocational and Generic Training Planning Team. Unpublished report, NPWP, Pretoria.
14. Sapere D. (1993), *Op cit.*
15. NPWP (1995), *Op cit.*

CHAPTER 12

Institution building for small-scale contractor development in South Africa

J. Ward

Background

During the 1960s and 1970s, black contractors in South Africa were constrained by racially biased restrictions to such an extent that normal development was impossible. Despite this despotic restriction of entrepreneurial spirit, the small-scale black contractor achieved some degree of emergence, particularly in the field of black-owned private housing developments within the restrictive township boundaries. Another route was for a black contractor to become a sub-contractor to a white contractor, often a 'front man' (hardly ever a 'front woman'). This gave the African limited access to work in the white residential areas.

In the view of Eric Miller, the primary task of a development programme is to help the client system to increase its control of its environment (including the local physical environment and the external environment that comprises the wider socio-economic-political system).[1]

Khuphuka: a case study

Khuphuka is a non-governmental, non-profit organization that was established in 1992 to assist in the development of disadvantaged communities throughout the province of KwaZulu Natal, although mainly within the Durban Functional Region (DFR). Khuphuka fulfils its development role primarily through a range of human resource development and training interventions, by facilitating the establishment of community-based facilities, and by stimulating job creation opportunities. With available statistics indicating that the rate of unemployment in the DFR is in the vicinity of 55 per cent, the absorptive capacity of the formal employment sector is low, so Khuphuka has concentrated mainly on encouraging employment opportunities in the community development and micro-enterprise ('informal') sectors.[2]

Khuphuka offers a wide range of skills training, including bricklaying, carpentry, plastering, plumbing, painting and decorating, and electrical installation trades. The approach can be described as 'training-through-production' using competency-based modular training (CBMT), and is implemented in a manner that integrates training into the production environment so that trainees practise their newly-learnt skills and attain industry norms and standards. Training is offered both on site and at Khuphuka's headquarters training facility in Congella. Because it also operates production units, with clients and customers determining quality standards, the 'training-through-production' methodology ensures that real competencies are achieved.

Training for self-employment

Project-based training to enable local people to work on development programmes such as clinics, schools, and roads will not necessarily enable them to obtain sustainable long-term employment. Training for these projects generally focuses on vocational and technical skills rather than the skills needed to establish and manage a small enterprise. In the light of the levels of unemployment in the country, it is not realistic to assume that many of these people will be able to obtain employment in the formal sector. Moreover, the nature of these projects means that employment is obtainable only during the limited period of construction, as the people employed on the project are eventually retrenched and there is no continuing demand for their limited skills. Khuphuka believes that enterprise training is also required to assist them to create jobs for themselves utilizing the technical skills that they have learned. Self-employment is the only realistic chance most of these people have of ensuring that they get sustainable jobs.

Based on varied experience in facilitating non-formal education and development, Khuphuka has concluded that the training needs of local 'grass-roots' participants (as opposed to their formal education needs) appear to lie at three generic levels:

○ the need to equip community groups with the organizational and managerial skills to control their own development competently, as well as to establish appropriate institutional structures

○ the need for technical skills to encourage local people to facilitate job-creation opportunities, to enable them to assimilate various technologies competently, and to construct and maintain community and other facilities (such as meeting halls, houses or school classrooms)

○ the need for business skills (how to operate a business, bookkeeping, marketing skills and so on) to enable local people with the necessary technical skills to provide job opportunities for themselves on a self-employment basis.

The construction industry offers a good range of small-scale enterprise opportunities for people with a good mix of basic technical and business skills.

Building sub-contracting, electrical construction installations, and cement block production are but a few of the entrepreneurial opportunities that arise in this regard. In this last area graduates with recently developed technical skills would be well placed to create sustainable job opportunities for themselves. Khuphuka's Enterprise Development Programme seeks to enable selected individuals and groups to gain access to appropriate training and support services.

The enterprise development programme (EDP)

With the emphasis of the Government of National Unity's Reconstruction and Development Programme (RDP) being on the built environment, a range of community development projects (such as clinics, community centres, crèches, housing and schools) need to built, as far as possible by local people. The EDP aims to help local people undertaking such projects, as well as providing material inputs. Khuphuka specifically appreciates the need for people to have access to a range of enterprise development training systems and methodologies to suit the special needs of small-scale construction and manufacturing enterprises. With these needs in mind, Khuphuka plans to develop a range of services to support its proposed training, consultancy and advisory activities for the small and micro-enterprise sector in general, and the small-scale construction and manufacturing sector in particular.

Khuphuka recognizes that training alone is not enough and, once trainees graduate from training programmes, Khuphuka's production units provide a temporarily protected market by using producer groups as sub-contractors in their operations until they are able to stand on their own. Support to these groups could include advice on sources of funding, organizational development, further training in both technical and business skills, co-operative buying schemes and access to markets. Sub-contracting also enables Khuphuka to take on larger contracts, thereby increasing its production and training capacity.

Training young adults

The target group is young adults (defined as people between the ages of 18 and 35) from disadvantaged backgrounds (of whom 30 per cent in total should be women) who often already have a level of technical skill (such as bricklaying, welding or carpentry) and have a desire to establish and/or to grow their own business. Khuphuka focuses specifically on supporting the establishment and growth of manufacturing enterprises (making items such as tables, cement block moulds, and light fittings), construction enterprises (small contractors and sub-contractors in both the building and civils/infrastructure fields), and service enterprises (such as domestic appliance repairs and building maintenance). While retail and small wholesaler enterprises generally have fewer barriers to entry (requiring little in the way of technical skills, a low asset base, less working capital, and so on), the scope for achieving sustainable employment growth in petty commodity trading is generally very limited.

The general profile sought by Khuphuka in emerging enterprises/entrepreneurs is as follows:

○ mainly individuals (although about 5 per cent could comprise community co-operative ventures)

○ a target gender balance of 70 per cent male and 30 per cent female (although a 50-50 split would be ideal)

○ a strong urban bias (80 per cent urban to 20 per cent rural)

○ the majority of the enterprises assisted should be related in some way or another to development projects such as schools (where, for example, a cement block enterprise has been established), a road (where, for example, a community gabion production co-operative has been assisted), or a bus-shelter project (where, for example, a metal work group has been established)

○ about 40 per cent of the enterprises in manufacturing, with a similar proportion of construction contractors, about 10 per cent wholesalers or retailers, with the remaining 10 per cent representing a mix of services, other commerce, and so on

○ mostly non-formal and unregistered (up to 80 per cent), with not more than 20 per cent formal, licensed, and tax-paying businesses.

An integrated programme

In terms of practical project-specific support, there are often opportunities to manufacture material items such as concrete block, bricks, door and window frames, and pine-batten doors. These enterprises can then be left as going concerns after the project is finished. Khuphuka aims to provide or co-ordinate the following five functions in an integrated programme.

Business and enterprise training

This comprises a range of business courses for individuals and groups with differing levels of formal education and operating in different sectors, such as bookkeeping, costing and pricing, customer relations and business financing.

Small-scale loan and revolving credit facility

Access to finance (by both the formal and non-formal banking systems) is facilitated by co-ordinating support to emerging and small enterprises. It is envisaged that the provision of small loans to specific graduate trainees (particularly those with proven technical expertise but little collateral) will be made available through access to revolving credit. It is envisaged that, subject to safeguards, such credit will be increased as the previous amount is repaid and the business demonstrates financial responsibility.

With respect to entrepreneur finance, Khuphuka intends to:

○ assist in establishing credit lines for small-scale enterprises (especially in the construction and manufacturing sectors). This would enable small contractors to have access to funds for initial seed capital as well as to meet surety requirements, and could take the form of a revolving fund
○ locate and interact with local small enterprise financing agencies
○ provide financial consultancy, advisory and counselling services.

The criteria for accessing loans is set by the financial institution, but a recommendation on the individual or group concerned can be provided by Khuphuka on the basis of their achievements in production-based training. Individuals wishing to acquire a loan should in general have completed a relevant business course, have compiled a suitable business plan for the enterprise, have paid their training course fees punctually, and have a bank (savings) account.

Enterprise information and support service
Khuphuka has found that emerging businesses frequently lack a reliable source of advice to deal with specific problems, such as the contractual implications of signing a lease agreement, negotiating a bank overdraft, or industrial relations. Thus it plans to provide an advisory service, by telephone in the first instance, backed up by a small documentation centre and research in the form of needs-analysis studies.

Enterprise projects
It aims to initiate and co-ordinate the establishment of a range of co-operative and other enterprises. These projects will relate largely to material inputs on building and infrastructure projects, and could include such enterprises as cement block and brick yards and the manufacture of wooden and/or metal door and window frames.

Contractor training and development programme
The object of this programme is to enhance, through training and mentoring, the management skills of small-scale construction entrepreneurs, enabling them confidently to become a part of the reconstruction and development of the revitalized construction sector. In essence, this provides the four above-mentioned functions (business training, facilitating access to business finance, one-on-one consulting and advice, and facilitating sub-contracting and other enterprise projects) in a sector-specific sub-unit, as well as developing and implementing a 'train-the-trainer' programme so that skills development can be facilitated country-wide.

Conclusions

The institutional and project cases illustrate the capacity of a new NGO to react flexibly and rapidly to national problems and opportunities. Khuphuka seeks to be entrepreneurial in its approach to helping emerging entrepreneurs, drawing upon existing national and international training material and experience where it is available, and working in partnership with other agencies wherever possible.

This approach meets the key concerns regarding contractor support agencies which is that *'institution building has become a popular pastime among development agencies, but costly bureaucracies are easier to create than to kill'*.[3] Perhaps the overwhelming advantage of the NGO vis-à-vis the public sector agency is that it ends quite simply when the flow of resources dries up. It is therefore forced to be entrepreneurial in seeking out new opportunities once the current demand for its services is met. Because NGOs generally lack a guaranteed long-term source of income, they are by nature client-oriented, and hence teach their client entrepreneurs to be client-oriented by example. It is too early to judge whether Khuphuka will be successful in working itself out of a job, but it does at least start with the advantage of recognizing that its task is to enable its client entrepreneurs to achieve autonomy.

References

1. Miller, Eric (1993) *From Dependency to Autonomy: Studies in Organization and Change,* Free Association Books, London
2. Winsnip, Guy (1995) 'Khuphuka Skills Training and Employment Programme: Small and Micro-Enterprise Development Funding Proposal', Khuphuka, Durban (unpublished)
3. Miles D. and Ward J. (1991) *Small Scale Construction Enterprises in Ghana: Practices, Problems and Needs,* ILO Construction Information Paper CIP/1, Geneva

Annexe A

Project Case Study - The Winterveld Presidential Project

The application of Khuphuka's approach to enterprise development is exemplified by a current project to deliver potable water to dwellings in the disadvantaged area of Winterveld. In line with the government's Reconstruction and Development Programme and the Public Works programme, the project aims to maximize job creation. Since this project is concerned with the laying of a pipeline throughout the township, jobs are created through the excavation and backfilling of pipe trenches, using labour-based technology.

The objective is to improve the living standards and quality of life of the community of Winterveld through:

○ development of human resources, by training new entrants to the construction process and existing small-scale contractors within the community
○ facilitating their entry into the formal construction contracting process
○ enabling them to acquire the skills necessary to become proficient and self-supporting engineering contractors
○ creating appropriate and cost-effective employment opportunities in the construction process
○ construction of the water supply scheme in Winterveld.

The programme has four main objectives:

1. To enable contractors to submit realistic tenders for construction contracts on the project.
2. To impart practical construction management skills to contractors, so that they can better organize their companies to become profitable.
3. To deliver appropriate skills and develop entrepreneurs in the community to sustain the project and job opportunities.

Table 12.1: Winterveld: Preliminary contract levels and conditions

Level	Assessment of skills and experience	Maximum contract value in rand ($ 1.00 = R 3.65)	Performance guarantees
A	Some ability to organize. Limited artisan skill.	Cost of labour component, including contractor's mark-up and profit, to a maximum value of R 10 000.	Not required
B	Established artisan. Civil engineering ganger, chargehand, gang boss.	Cost of labour component, including contractor's mark-up and profit, to a maximum value of R 40 000.	Not required
C	Advanced gang or trade managerial ability.	Total contract price, to a maximum value of R 250 000.	Not required
D	Advanced general management ability. Commercial experience.	Total contract price, to a maximum value of R 850 000.	5 per cent of contract price
E	Advanced construction management ability. Marketing skills. Credibility with financial institutions.	Total contract price, to a maximum value of R 2 500 000.	10 per cent of contract price

4. To expand the future prospects of the contractors, particularly in the labour-based sector, by imparting to them the confidence, knowledge, skills and experience to bid for future contracts outside the Winterveld Residential Area.[1]

Recognizing the need to facilitate entry into the construction process by external participants as well as members of the Winterveld community, it was decided that there should be five progressively more testing levels of contract, A to E, the last being conventional construction contracts, see Table 12.1.[2] Another feature of the project was a partnership approach, with complementary objectives recognized both by the project managers and the participants in the programme, as described in Table 12.2.

Table 12.2: Winterveld: Complementary needs of project management and contractors

Needs of project management	Needs of contractors
1. To deliver approximately 130 successfully completed contracts, to a total value of R 35 million, within an 18-month project period.	1. To learn how to prepare and submit project-specific tenders.
2. To have the majority of these contracts executed by existing and emerging contractors from the Winterveld residential area, with the remainder executed by disadvantaged contractors from the townships in the immediate vicinity.	2. To learn how to prepare and submit standard and non-standard contract tenders, falling outside the scope of the project.
3. To support and encourage contractors to reach higher levels of classification throughout the project period.	3. To develop skills in: ○ Contracting ○ Administration ○ Money management ○ Construction management ○ Materials management
4. On the completion of the project, to select maintenance contractors for the upkeep of the water reticulation service.	4. To become part of the eventual operation and maintenance of the newly established services.
5. To give to those people previously excluded, the opportunity to enter the field of labour-based construction.	5. To build confidence in the ability to compete on an equal footing with conventional contractors, and to gain commercial credibility.

A phased training programme

The training programme was planned in two phases, the first of which was project-specific while the second phase was designed to provide the participating contractors with the skills that would be needed to compete in the open market.

Phase 1

Enabling contractors to submit realistic bids for Winterveld-specific contracts. In order to achieve this, training materials and methodology were based on contractor classification requirements from level B to level D, under the following sub-headings:

○ documentation
○ conditions of contract
○ job specifications
○ quality control
○ tender preparation and submission
○ tender adjudication
○ responsibilities of contractors
○ responsibilities of project management.

The Phase 1 courses were designed so as to be capable of being repeated as required throughout the duration of the project, so that the contractors could be progressively upgraded.

Phase 2

This was the major component of the business/construction management skills training for contractors at classification levels B, C, and D. Training methodology focuses on interactive group participation, so that the experience of the more senior contractors can be passed on to their emerging counterparts.

The trainers used the ILO Improve Your Construction Business (IYCB) training material, which the author had contributed to as co-author and had field tested during a period as chief technical adviser on an ILO field project in Ghana.[3] This material was specifically designed to suit small building and public works contractors in low- and middle-income countries, and lends itself to the highly participative approach which was preferred. It consists of the following titles:

1. Pricing and Bidding. Workbook and Handbook[4]
2. Site Management. Workbook and Handbook[5]
3. Business Management. Workbook and Handbook[6]

The level of impact of the learning methodology was closely monitored, based on the training assessment form illustrated in Figure 12.1, so that continuous improvement can be achieved through reassessment of needs on an ongoing basis.

The delivery of knowledge and the acquisition of new competencies was just the first stage of the learning process. Once these were successfully achieved, the next stage was the transfer of the theory learned to the actual managing of the contract. The final stage was a decision on whether the contractor was competent enough to be advanced to the next classification level, which was made jointly by the training manager and the construction manager.

References

1. Van Wyk and Louw Inc (1995), *Provisions and Procedures for the Invitation of Tenders and Quotations, Adjudication and Award of Contracts for the Winterveld Water Supply Project*, Van Wyk and Louw Inc. Pretoria

Training method	General awareness of new skills	Organized knowledge of underlying concepts and theory	Learning new skills	Application on the job
Presentation and description of new skills (e.g. lectures, site visits)				
Modelling the new skills (e.g. demonstrations)				
Practice in simulated setting (e.g. action exercises)				
Feedback on trainee performance in simulated and real settings.				
Coaching and hands-on assistance on the job.				

Figure 12.1 *Training impact assessment form*
Source: Ray Bolam

2. Van Wyk and Louw Inc (1995), *Project Document for 7.5 km of Pipeline and Appurtenant Works*, Van Wyk and Louw Inc. Pretoria.
3. Miles, D. and Ward, J. (1991), *Small-scale Construction Enterprises in Ghana: Practices, Problems and Needs*, ILO Construction Information Paper CIP/1, Geneva.
4. Andersson, C., Miles, D., Neale, R. and Ward, J. (1994*), Improve Your Construction Business Handbook 1 and Workbook 1 - Pricing and Bidding*, International Labour Office, Geneva.
5. Andersson, C., Miles, D., Neale, R. and Ward, J. (1995*), Improve Your Construction Business Handbook 2 and Workbook 2 - Site Management*, International Labour Office, Geneva.
6. Andersson, C., Miles, D. and Ward, J. (1995), *Improve Your Construction Business Handbook 3 and Workbook 3 - Business Management*, International Labour Office, Geneva.